Campaign page views per day

Tracking daily campaign page views can help you monitor the effectiveness of your efforts.

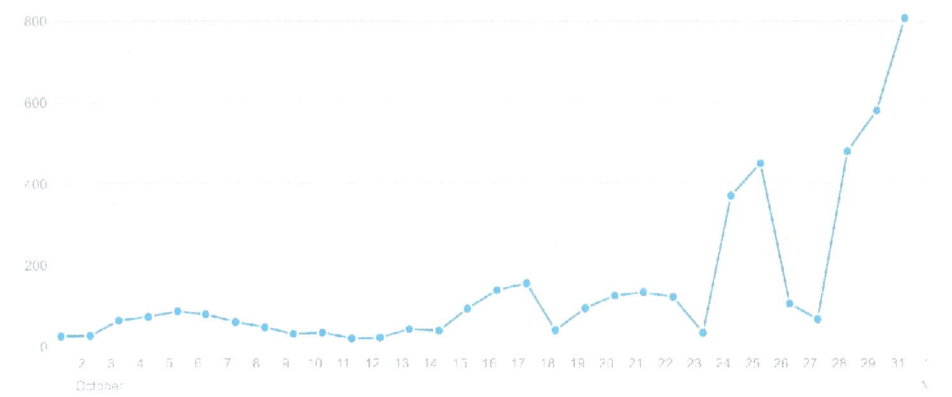

DO YOU FANCY A $25000 PUBLISHING DEAL?

Written By

Elina Salajeva

How to Secure a Publishing Contract with Amazon Kindle Scout worth $25000

How to Run an Effective KDP Kindle Scout Book Promotion?

The road to become a Millionaire.

Case Study: The Girl with the Tiger Tattoo and the Magnificent 6

Do You Want a Five-year Publishing Contract?

Worth $25000 with a cash advancement of $1500?

Does That Sound Fabulous!

Buy This Book NOW!!

Witten by

Elina Salajeva

Overview

Imagine winning that lucrative contract worth $25 000 in five-years and a cash advancement of $1500 and lifetime royalties of 70%. Does that sound great? Surely that should for any serious-money-minded person. Amazon has given every author an opportunity to strike it big. The idea is simple write a book, upload it and go on a mind-boggling campaign for 30 days. Sell your book's idea, promote it whichever way you want and at the end of a 30-day campaign reap the rewards and be awarded a lucrative contract worth thousands of dollars. Sounds simple, does it?

If it sounds that simple but why so many are failing to secure that lucrative contract. Are you thinking of writing a book and enter it into the Kindle Scout program? Have you entered already and you are under-performing? Have you already failed securing that lucrative contract? Now look no further this book is the answer to all your miseries and failures. If you are serious about securing that lucrative contract with Amazon, then look no further. Buy this book like yesterday, time waits for no man. Buy the book now! This will be your best buy of 2016 trust me. This book has methods and suggestions to make it easy for anyone to have a big chance of being awarded that contract. I have used a case study to home down the point. *The Girl with the Tiger Tattoo and the Magnificent 6*, a book I recently wrote and was published by Amazon. I have recently been in the Kindle Scout program so whatever I am telling you is tried and trusted and I can prove that my methods work. Don't waste time you have one opportunity with every book. I know it can take up to 6 months to write just one book so why take an unnecessary risk of going through the 30-day campaign without reading my book. If you were a soldier would you go to war without a gun? A big No? So, buy this book and read it now in the end you will thank me.

I can tell you that my method is unique, and you will love it. I have managed to reach campaign page views per day of more than 800. I have researched everywhere to see if anyone has been hitting figures like that before, but it seems so far I am the only one who understand the principle behind this. This is a fact buy the book you will see for yourself that the methods in this book have never been used before in promotion and publishing circles.

If you are seriously about securing that lucrative contract buy this book today and start that life changing campaign. The methods in this book are simple and straight forward. They require a certain amount of creativeness from you and you should think outside the box and outside your comfort zone. To succeed you need to prove that you are a cut-above-the rest. You must show that you have the stamina and hunger to promote your book and lay that foundation for future customers and your success. You should be able to sell your ideas. You should be able to convince others to support you. You should have excellent skills and use the social networks to your advantage. You must have excellent communication skills as well to be able to persuade supporters to nominate your book. The processes in this book requires one to be very flexible and adapt to changing circumstances. Don't go with the flow, the methods can only work depending on your attitude. Don't go with the flow, take things into your control and aim to influence the outcome. Don't be like most of the people, they wait for the perfect time to come around so that they can start embarking on their dream project. Instead you chase after that opportunity.

Look at the big picture, imagine you are the publisher yourself and someone gave you their book to promote. You are buying the book today for $1500 cash and $25000 to be paid five years down the line. Would you like an "exhausted-tired" book that nearly lost its flavour or you would want a hot book just the day before you publish it. Wouldn't it be nice to publish the book today when there are 800 potential customers ready to buy it? Or you would prefer to start searching for all those people who were interested in the book the first week you launched your promotional campaign. In short it's all about understanding the idea behind all this. It's about strategizing. Don't just throw everything in, at the beginning like what most people are doing right now. Sit down plan everything and see your plans through. Clearly define what you are trying to achieve, and plan for the resources needed to carry out that task and think big and enjoy the campaign. I would like to be paid doing what I love to do. You are an author, this what you are good at so enjoy promoting your book and have fun. Don't do like most of the people who from day one lose scope of what they are trying do by going for nominations instead of selling their book to potential customers. Most authors entering the Kindle Scout program don't realise that there are there to lay a strong fan base for their book. It's not just a matter of seeking nominations. If you do it right nominations comes naturally after you have built a strong supporter base. So, this Kindle Scout program is a way of laying your foundation for your book readers, for your book supporters and for your loyal fan base. So, it's wrong to start day one with a request for nominations from a stranger before you get to know them. Be polite these people are like you too. Get to know them first, introduce yourself, introduce your book let them know you will be happy for them to fall in love with your book. Explain also that you are being considered for a publishing contract and that their feedback would be greatly appreciated. Give them a day or two for them to look at your book's excerpt. But let them know you will need their feedback. After a day or two then ask for their support and if they can nominate your book. In that way, you will have built trust, honesty and integrity all fundamental in the long-term relationship between them and your book.

The Girl with the Tiger tattoo and the Magnificent 6

Elina Salajeva

In a world where to serve and to protect and honor means more than life itself.

Can You Escape Your Destiny ?

01/11/2016   Kindle Scout

How It Works   Your Campaigns   Your Scout Profile   [Search Kindle Scout | Go]   Hello, Elina
Your Account

Browse by **Category**   Your **Nominations**

BACK TO YOUR CAMPAIGNS

Campaign Stats for *The Girl with the Tiger tattoo and the Magnificent 6.*

You can use this data to learn a little more about your Scouts and refine your outreach strategy. We update these stats every day.

Last updated: November 1, 2016 at 5:11 AM EDT

0
Ended

Start date: October 2, 2016
End date: November 1, 2016

Hours in Hot & Trending
48 of 720

Total campaign page views
4.4K

Hours in Hot & Trending per day

The Hot & Trending list can give you a sense of your book's popularity with readers.

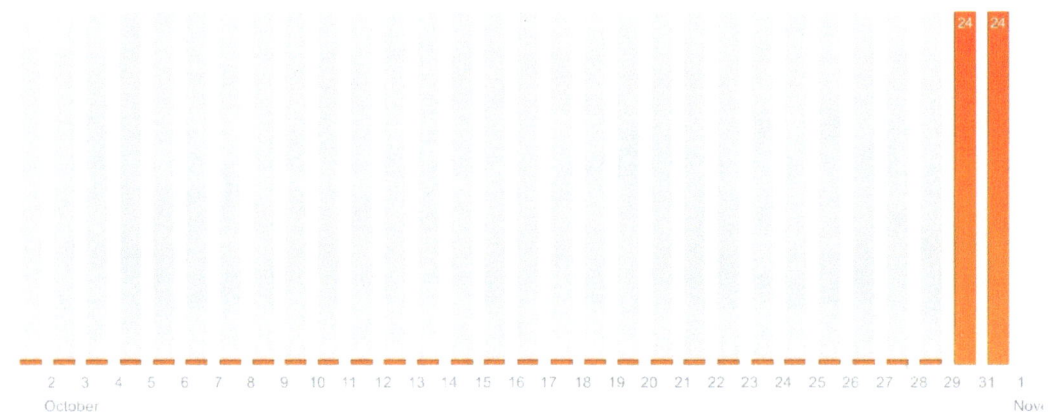

Campaign page views per day

Tracking daily campaign page views can help you monitor the effectiveness of your efforts.

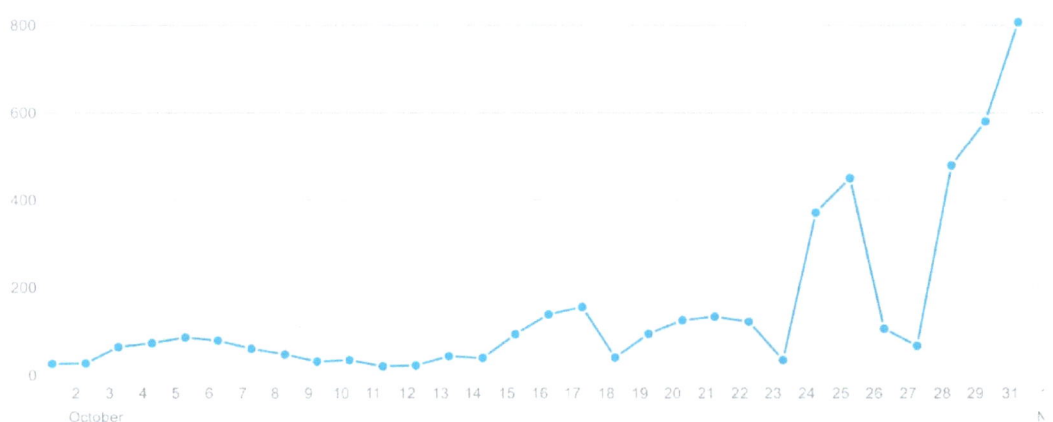

https://kindlescout.amazon.com/author/project/1N5BYLN9OGELY/campaign-data   1/3

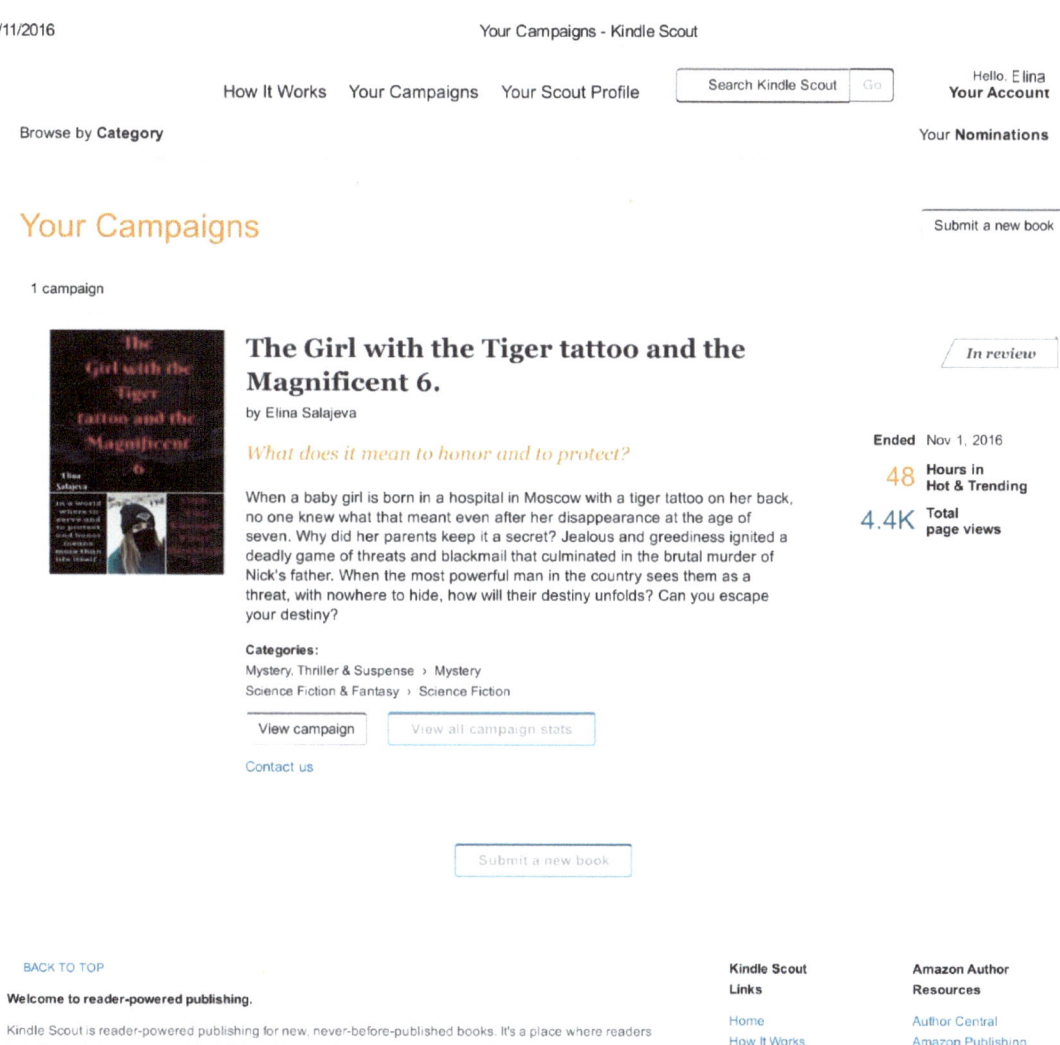

Background.

How to Run an effective KDP Kindle Scout Book Promotion:

Case study; The Girl with The Tiger Tattoo and the Magnificent 6

Fancy a five-year publishing contract worth $25 000 and a $1500 cash advance? Does that sound great? Surely this should be, I tell you it's not easy but it can be done. This book is full of ideas and tried and trusted methods to just do that. The Gold rush for the eBooks especially the kindle book is on-right now. Just imagine what it will be like in a few years' time, the paper book will be like the cassette tapes being replaced by the cheaper CDs or the Cds being replaced by the MP3s, the iPod and iPads. Just imagine being able to sell copies of your books for the rest of your life. Imagine making up to 70% of commission as royalties through Amazon. This sounds great but imagine also selling your book to billions of customers worldwide, does that not arouse your interest and imagination? Certainly, that will for any serious-money making minded person. The big question is; How then it is hard to become a billionaire if it sounds that easy?

Given that kindle books have gone global why is it hard to become a billionaire overnight. I have known people who have been publishing books now but they haven't become millionaires just from kindle book sales. Over the years I have studied systems and how most companies for example fail to make billions of sales revenues despite selling in global markets where they have potential of selling to billions. I wrote a book entitled Brexit Aftermath: What is the way forward a book one should read to understand how these systems work globally. This is a deep analysis of how the systems in the whole world works be it locally or globally. Once one understands this then will one be able to make huge profits through book sales. Most people think that it's a matter of writing a book and publishing it and then sit and relax hoping that millions of dollars will roll into your bank account. There are millions of writers and publishers out there all fighting for a share of these billion dollars. Is it easy to make $ millions or $ billions? I have read countless articles on the internet on how to become a millionaire written by people who have not sold millions themselves. Nothing will stop you from becoming a billionaire overnight but I am just saying it's not easy as the people think. The last article I read on internet pertains to an author who wrote a book and published it on Amazon website. For more than 6 months no one had bought the book. There were loads of free-books on downloads but with nothing to show for it as his bank account had no money from his kindle book sales. He had tried all kinds of book promotions, advertising his book on many websites and doing everything he can to promote his book. Still there was nothing to show for it. Months later when he changed his understanding of the system, understanding on how things work did he start making money. In this book, I am going to show you how best to make a lot of money in the nearby future. It's not easy as people put it but It can be achieved if one follows the methods and guidelines in this book.

The world over the past years has been evolving and the methods of doing things had changed and evolved too. But years after years' man has tended to go back to the past to seek for the future. In that case methods of doing things had not changed much the ideas are still the same but just refined and adapted to suit the local conditions. History after history we have seen mankind implement the ideas that worked in the beginning of time and over the years these ideas have been refined and made fit for the local conditions and beliefs but the principle is still the same. Many companies, countries and international organisation all employ the same idea as the man in the beginning of time. These methods were tried and trusted up to now they still work. The idea is the same no matter how you want to look at it. To be big you must be, first creative and secondly you must take risks. There is a link between creativity and risk taking making it big.

Risk taking
Riches

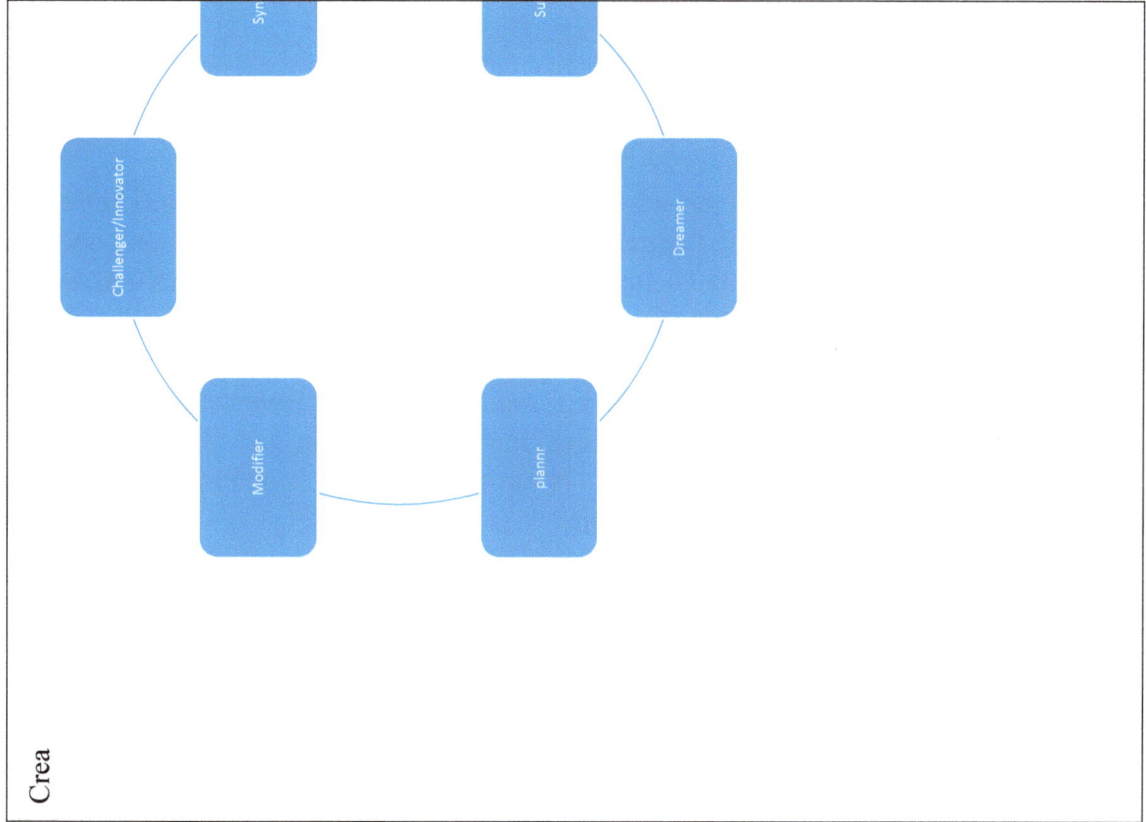

Creativity

Taking the honey bees colony for example they all live together in well-organized colonies where everyone else participate for the better meant of the whole group. They have successful colonies because they have excellent communication among themselves. Everything is well planned and organised they have certain bees responsible for nest construction, others responsible for defence and others for labour. A close look at each colony will quickly reveal that they have a queen, workers and drones. The colony depends on effective communication and teamworking. Everything is done in the name of the colony. Everyone else work for the betterment of a colony. This is a social way of life everything for the common good of others and everyone concerned.

Anything collected be it food or otherwise is shared and is for the common good of everyone concerned. There are rules and regulations that must be obeyed for the common good of the colony. The whole process is for the betterment of the colony. There are no individual preferences and any rivalries are killed off by the queen bee. Everyone works for the better of the whole colony. Looking at the diagram above you will see that most bees fall under the Dreamer, the Sustainer and the Planner. The bee workers and the drones all have roles which are essential to the survival of the colony. Their decision-making powers are limited, what they can do individually is limited too. Whatever they do is limited to support, planning, and sustaining roles. All their lives their work to support the colony.

Looking at the above bee colony and the above graph where would you fit today? Are you the Dreamer? Are you the Sustainer? Or you are the planner? For some they form under the modifier and the synthesizer. To be honest for most of you, taking it or leaving it you all fall under the three bottom categories. You are either the dreamer, the planner or just the Sustainer there to sustain the system without any major impact. You are there to support the system so that the system develops and expands smoothly. You play a major role and that's about it, you will write books after books but achieving greatness in terms of revenue from sales will be limited. This is not because of the bee colony itself. No. Don't blame the colony. The colony itself has nothing to do with your failures. Please don't mis-quote me tomorrow any say I wrote that it's the colonies fault. I am saying the colony is an entity in its own with its rules to protect its survival and growth and prosperity. It provides opportunities for you as a bee to live a better life and survive. The colony provides a lot of opportunities and benefits for you.

The colony provides protection. There are others to help you, there are others to offer support and protection in case you need it. Just like in a bee colony you all work together to sustain the colony and get food and life essential in return. You will never make much because first, the colony has rules that prohibits self-greediness. This in turn restricts on the things you can claim as yours free from any member of the colony. Your role, nor matter how hard this might be to swallow, your role is to sustain the development of the colony and its growth and survival.

For the colony to survive and grow there are rules within the bee colony where each one must observe to be accepted as a member of the colony. Everyone must work for the benefit of the colony. There are no self-oriented goals. You either obey the rules or leave the colony if you are lucky not to be killed. The rules are there to avoid creating other colonies within the colony. The rules are to make sure that first the colony operates smoothly without any rivalry. Any instability can mean the end of the colony. The queen bee is there to eliminate any rivalry if another female bee remains in the colony. They can stay only if they don't draw much attention. The rules of the colony are there to make sure the colony survives and functions smoothly. Therefore, in the graph above there are fewer Modifiers, Synthesizers, Innovators and Challengers in a bee colony. Why? This is for the smooth operation of the colony. This guarantees the survival and growth of the colony. In life, this is also true of many organisation and companies and societies. The lack of Modifiers, Challengers and Innovators in a bee colony means the smooth operation of the colony, everyone must work for the common good. Most of the people don't think outside the box. Most bees don't think outside the colony. There are there to make sure that the colony survives and runs smoothly. Look at the diagram above again. What position would you put yourself in today if you were in the bee colony. Would you be Worker bee or a drone. In other words, are you a Dreamer, a Sustainer or a Planner. The idea is to strive to be a Synthesizers, to be a Modifier, to be a Challenger and an Innovator and a Leader that's where the big bucks are.

The idea is not to challenge the colony. The idea is not to fight the colony. The idea is not to disobey the rules. Most people have tended to oppose the colonies in the bee world. They have revolted against such practises. Wars had been fought in the past. All this is a misconception. They say if you can't stand the heat then get out. The main idea which I will stress throughout the whole book is not to try and change others tried and trusted methods. The bees have developed this strategy of growth and survival for millions of years. It works and this is for the common good of the colony. The idea is not to fight others' ideas.

The idea here is to starting THINKING BIG THINK GLOBAL BUT ACTING LOCALLY.

Empires, countries and companies have all adopted this approach and survived millions of years. The main point in this book is for you to START THINKING BIG AND START THINKING GLOBALLY. My father said to me one day; "My daughter you know what, the best things all come from nature. Those who listen and understand nature are the greatest innovators". At that time, it didn't make any sense I just thought here we go again one of his rumblings after a drinking session but years later I have noticed that everything man has done better, everything man has developed and innovated has its origins in nature. For every best design, there is always a counterpart in nature. Planes like birds, animal in the world living like humans in societies. Best survival and social cohesion groups are found in nature in the form of bees. Most companies are modelled after bee's colonies for them to survive and grow. Look at lion prides there is only one male lion and everyone else follows the rules of the leader for the pride to survive. Whenever there is a rival lion the leader of the head will fight and kill the rival because no divided attention and resources. Imagine that the other rivalry lion what to set up its own pride within the pride. There will be divided resources, there will be competition, there will be fighting, there is no way the two groups can equally gain resources, the resources will be split into two groups now they must share what they gain from a hunt. Surely this will disadvantage the original male lion. So, for the optimum gains the alpha lion will impose rules so that whatever benefits are derived from a hunt are equally shared and for the benefit of his pride for his survival and wellbeing of the pride. This is true for every organisation, company or country. This is life unless you start thinking at the big picture you can write many books but you will not make any impact. WHY? Because you haven't read this book. So, do you want to make billions when the time comes. The gold rush of kindle books is ahead of us. There are opportunities ahead of us but the question is;

First. Will you notice the opportunities when they arrive?

Second. Will you be prepared to receive them by both hands?

Thirdly. Will you be the few who think outside the box?

Fourthly. Will you understand nature and look for example from nature to exceed or you will be there to sustain others without any real impact.

Fifthly. Will you have the stamina and flexibility to adapt to ever changing needs and wants.

This book is the Holy grain of Kindle marketing. Read the book and use the guidelines and start acting today to become a global kindle seller. The idea here which has worked for me and which with no doubt will work for you is to look at all this from a different perspective. Stop going with the flow. Start thinking at nature for all your answers. Stop fighting and destroying others well established colonies or ideas. Start thinking big and start thinking globally. I have read numerous stories of companies that started in the backyard garden but which are now a global force. There are no miracles in all of them. It's sheer realization that you must think big and think global. Take any example you like, for every one of them it is simply the idea of expanding that presented opportunities which they were prepared to take with both hands. Imagine all those kings and Emperors who have sacrificed thousands of their best soldiers just to have a larger country or more territories, were they mad? Look at Alexander the great he spent most of his life trying to create the greatest empire. He knew you must think big and think globally. That brings me to point number two. The idea here is to learn and understand and not to challenge already established colonies or companies. Learn from others to achieve greatness. If you can't stand the heat in the kitchen you get out of the kitchen. If you can't fight them then join them. The most important factor here is to form your own entity, start your own colony independent of all major players. Rely on them but on a different capacity or level. This cannot be achieved overnight but start working towards independence and forming partnership links with all major players. See yourself as the leader, start thinking like you are on the top of the colony. You are now the leader and there are people in your network, in your colony who depend on you. You must set up rules that ensures the survival of your own colony. Rules which will make sure that you will be the only leader within your colony. Remove any competition within your colony. Make sure that you have clearly defined goals and objectives for your colony. Set rules and implement these to make sure that your colony survives and runs smoothly. Therefore, think big think globally but act locally. For most people, they think wow no way, when they hear the word global but it shouldn't be like that. Always think global but act local. This is true just look at all this as a large scale of your local project. Adjust where necessary to local conditions. First and foremost, there are key attributes you need to have or learn or adopt to be successful. Rule number one think and act like the leader. Be your own boss never look at anyone else for answers instead have the answers on your fingertips.

Think like a leader as you are now one and act like one too. You now have your own colony to run smoothly and make sure that everyone works for your benefit and the benefits of the rest so that the colony is sustained over time. Therefore, you must have the following qualities and attributes.

To succeed you must have or strive to adopt these qualities.

Great Vision

Just like the leaders of any country or organisation have a clear vision and understanding of what you are trying to achieve. Clearly define your goals and set up your objectives. You can be ambitious it won't hurt but be realistic as possible. Set achievable goals. You must be able at least to achieve certain objectives and goals within the short run. Have long term goals that are part and complimentary to the short-term goals. The long plan can be to sell your book in 60 different countries by 2026 and yearly you must have short term goals in relationship with the long-term goals.

Effective Communication Skills

To be a successful billionaire selling kindle books communication is a major attribute as your success depends on it. Any successful campaign depends on your communication skills. You are the leader, are you able to put your message across. This is not just the skill of delivering the message this is the communication between you the leader and everyone concerned. You are now the centre piece the solution to all problems and the main reason that the company or your colony exist. You can be just you but think yourself as your own boss. You must know who to ask, who to approach and who to form partnerships with. You must communicate with everyone concerned through various methods, without this it will be a great challenge to go global.

You must be focused.

Have clearly defined goals and remain focused until the goals and objectives are realized. You must know what you want to achieve. Have plans drawn down and stay focused. Be flexible but stay on course when the tough gets going.

Innovativeness

You must be very much interested in thinking of better ways to achieve results. You must focus on new techniques and think of better ways to market your book and expand. You must look at nature and try to think outside the box. Nature has all the answers look at what will work best for help there are always modern day techniques corresponding to ideas in nature. Look at migratory birds for example when it's winter in one country or region they travel long distances to other regions for food comfort and to lay eggs. Look at the chameleon for example when presented with challenges and or threats it changes colour. That brings me to another point when I was promoting my book; "The Girl with the Tiger Tattoo and the Magnificent 6". The picture I placed on one of the adverts as the main cover was declined on another advertising platform. This was because the original cover image had too much text. At the last minute, I chose a slightly different cover image. In the end, I ended up with two different but similar campaigns and noticed that other target customers were avoiding the first image but preferring the second image. In the end, I ended up with a book with the main cover and a page just after with the second cover image so that both readers knows that it's the same book. This is part of thinking globally but acting locally. You are the main boss your own leader so be very creative. Don't just say that all traditional books have one cover why should I create a book with two covers. The second book can be a transparent paper with the second image of the book. Whatever it is try to be innovative.

Passionate

I love writing and I have always shown my passion even when I was kid. I don't care about some things but when it comes to writing I show real enthusiasm, that helps a lot. In short you must love what you do. You must be 100% committed and passionate about what you do. You must have the passion to push for more even if you are doing well. You must be hungry for more, pushing for better and bigger. In whatever you do show your passion. It's the idea of making big money that should drive you and show your passion so that it's easy to win others. It's easy to succeed in something you are passionate about. You will always put that much-needed extra effort just because you are doing things you love to do.

Persistence

You should also read my book called Chase Your Dreams and Never Give Up on kindle. Persistence is the key to success. There are failures in the real world. There are many obstacles in the real world. To succeed you must get up quickly after a setback. They say iterative development which involves a great deal of persistence plus creativity is equals to innovation. Persistence here will refer to the continual searching, development and testing together with creativity that will lead to innovation. Have the stamina to get up after a fall. Always start again after a failure have the energy to carry own. Persistently and systematically always see your plans through.

Be a strong decision maker.

The idea here is for one to see himself or herself as the leader and no one else. Avoid dependency, work harder and smarter. Strive to come up with ideas and solutions. Leaders make effective decisions they think and focus on innovations. They have the ability and willingness to think beyond short term goals and needs. Leaders resist the temptation to cut back or reduce resources that feeds research and development and innovation. They have a positive mindset and likewise be strong willed in making decisions. Don't procrastinate otherwise opportunities will pass you. The most misconception is that people think that after publishing their book own Amazon kindle Scout or other platforms they will sit down and relax and let Amazon do the rest. Ok there is no doubt Amazon will use their influence and customer base to promote your book. But if you are serious about real bucks take the bull by the horns and start thinking outside the box. Start viewing Amazon as a trading partner. There is a whole chapter on this issue in my other book called Brexit: Aftermath. What is the way forward? This brings me to the main argument in this book and the challenge I am posing to you the reader. Most policies adopted by these organisation and successful companies are there to steer the growth of the colony, company or organisation. The idea is not to create small niche millionaires or billionaires within their colonies or organisations but to see the rapid growth of these organisations and companies. The organisation or company concerned will reward you what they think will be enough for you which is normally a fraction of what they actual get. No organisation would survive and grow if it had to share equally everything they get. They offer you a percentage of what they get based on their efforts and strategy. There is no doubt that they are challenging forces not to be taken for granted or misinterpreted. They have enormous benefits and bargaining power. Look at the EU for example they use the same principle. They make a single market where all you can trade independently without restrictions and taxes. They offer ready markets open to all globally. There is reduced taxes and easy access to billions of potential customers. The EU is a catalyst and springboard between member states and the rest of the world. No doubt they present good quality products and increased competition but main ideal is for their sustainable growth and development. Without these dreamers, planners and Sustainer the system will collapse and they will cease to exist. Therefore, they form and secure better deals that benefits their members and in return the members must abide by the rules to remain part of the organisation or colony.

Be the decision maker, try to be the first and when you make decisions make them on firm ground, show your confidence. To make it big start viewing others as partners start looking for partnership deals and agreement. Start thinking big start establishing links and relationships based on mutual trust. See yourself as equal partners yet complementary. They cannot do without you and you cannot do without them either. Establish good solid relationships built on trust and understanding.

Be optimistic and fearless

You must believe that whatever you want to do is achievable. You are now the leader you set the goals and objectives. You know what you want to achieve. You must be optimistic and believe that it's achievable. You must be fearless and be determined to play the game and win. There is no turning back. You are on your own therefore establish ambitious plans but be more realistic you don't want to be very much disappointed. Set achievable goals.

The rules to How to run an effective KDP Kindle Scout/book promotion campaign.

*Rule number One

Think and act like a leader now. See other major plays like your business partners. You now have all the answers don't look for anyone else for answers. Start looking to want the other market leaders are doing and tailor your efforts to suit your own strategy. Instead of relying on Amazon to market your books start viewing Amazon as a trending partner. Aim to secure deals with them to promote your books. View them as business partners. Start assuming you are all equal you have been to college together and they are your best friends. You need help you need their expertise, do you just let them run around for you for nothing? Or you will start thinking big. You start looking for ways to benefit you and them as well to establish trust and good working relationships. Instead of buying that expensive watch you saw from outside that expensive jewellery shop find a cheaper version that you will wear for next few weeks and try and save £100. Tell yourself you can't just rely on freebies. You want to be an equal partner and not a subordinate. Amazon can advertise your book globally for a minimum of £100 per advert. Be courage's and start thinking like a leader. The kindle book is yours start putting efforts yourself take control of your plans. Invest that £100 and benefit from that vast market Amazon has. Authors know it's hard to write books and everyone want to be paid just like Amazon they are providing a service so they expect to be paid too. Like the story I mentioned above of this gentleman who wrote a book and published it on Amazon. After six months, the only books that were downloaded were those he had offered for free during the free book campaign. After months, he thought of spending £100 on advertisement that's when his book started selling. People everywhere no matter what they do and how they earn a living they expect everyone to contribute somehow. It's a misconception that you will become a millionaire by just publishing your book and let Amazon do the rest. You must chip-in as well do your part and let them do what they are best at. Throw the £100 at them advertise your book. See them as your partner and work along them. Promote your book too when they are promoting your book. Ask for advice and support as you would to a partner.

*Rule number two

Think all your relationships with everyone concerned as one of mutual trust and understanding. Strive to establish sound working relationships. With yourself as not a subordinate but a mutual partner. The idea here is to work towards self-sufficient and independence. Establish relations and cultivate these over the years. Have the independence of having a say in things that affects your book and you as an author.

*Rule number three

Set a budget for running the adverts. You will need at least £100- £150 to spend over the 30days on adverts that generate interest and traffic to your website at the same time building a strong reliable customer base. You can opt to advertise for free in several websites and books that's your option but for me that alone is not enough. I am the kind of person who will not leave anything to chance I must take control of everything I do. To be sure and guaranteed great results have a budget set aside some money for advertising and promoting your book. This will be looked at in more detail in the coming chapters but you can set a budget to spend daily on adverts say £5 a day on Facebook. In other words, take control of the direction this will take or at least try to influence the outcome don't leave everything to chance.

*Rule number four

Think outside the box take control of the project, personally contact potential supporters and helpers and ask them to help with your campaign. Send personal invitations, introduce yourself, sell your idea convince them to support your campaign.

*Rule number five

Don't leave it until too late. Make hay whilst the sun is shining. The first weeks are crucial depending on your status within the industry. If you are new this will be challenging as you will need to gather supporters and followers first. It's easy if you are an already established author nevertheless open twitter account, Facebook account, Headtalker account, thunderclap account etc. Work very hard the first week gathering future supporters. Spread the word the first weeks, approach a lot of potential supporters the first one or two weeks.

Looking at the creativity and innovation relationship in the diagram below you will notice that there is a link between risk taking, being creative and success. (*Idea adopted from the creatrix analysis*). The bottom part is characterized by less risk taking and less creativity. Authors in this category are those authors who go with the flow. They work very hard writing the book once they have finished writing they leave everything to the publisher. They let the publisher do everything for them. They don't worry much after they have completed writing their book. Their job is done. They don't worry about promoting their book or advertising it as much as the others whom we are going to look at below. They are there to sustain the process to help the current norm and status quo. They can be referred to as the Sustainer or Dreamer because all they do is hope and hope that everything will be okay. They have great ideas and plans but rarely get involved, in other words they don't get their hands dirty. Unless they pay their publisher for services rendered then these authors will have a comfortable life but that's about it. They don't take risks they are not creative they go with the flow.

Then we have the Planners category. These authors have great ideas; they go one step ahead than the Sustainer and the Dreamers. They devise plans, they have dreams of making it big. They don't just sit and let the publisher do everything for them. Just like the Sustainer and the Dreamers below them in the end planning is all they can do with no tangible plans. They lack commitments and rarely set aside to kick start their plans. In the end, they are just like the Sustainer and the Dreamers in that their plans will gather dust with no commitment and implementation. They don't budget and rarely spend money on their campaigns. They utilize free advertisements with little or no impact on the outcome. They take a little bit of risk and in cooperate some creativity in their work.

The Modifiers take risks they invest money in their book campaigns but they are less creative. They try new things, new markets and incorporate new ideas. They are better than the Planners, the Sustainer and the Dreamers in that they actual take risks, they try new things they haven't tried before but they are less creative. The Synthesizer on the other hand take as much risks as the Modifiers trying new things and different forms of promoting their books. They go a further step than the Modifiers in that they are very creative and incorporate some creativity in the way they promote their books. Synthesizers try to be very creative they look at their surroundings and try to adopt things they like and introduce these to the way they advertise or promote their books. They adopt some aspects from their day to day life and try to adapt these to the way they promote their books. Their name is derived from the music Synthesizer. They generate a lot of different ideas from all walks of life and try to use these in their promotion. It's not surprising that these authors are often richer than the other four categories namely the Modifiers, the Planners, the Dreamer and the Sustainer respectively. They often enjoy doing this and find it easy to relate and connect with people because they incorporate skills, methods and ideas often associated with everyday life familiar with the people.

The Practicalizer takes risks and he is equally creative as well. These authors balance risk and creativity. They don't take more risk than they become more creativity. They are better than all the categorise mentioned so far. They earn high but not enough to make serious money. They are an advanced form of the Planners in that they take a lot of risk. They are usually the developed forms of the planners. They don't let their plans gather dust in the garage or somewhere. They strive to be different, they take risks but lack the creativity and resources to strike it big. They are very practical, they put everything into plans and follow detailed methods. This in the end will be their focus, they end up spending more time detailing their plans. They are very practical everything must follow previously defined methods and plans. You can easily see that they are not very creative as they focus on practical trusted methods and in the end, they don't break the barriers and make real money.

The challenger is creative and takes a lot of risks. They are more risks takers than they are creative. They are not afraid to put their ideas to paper and into action. They earn more than their efforts than the other groups mentioned above. They are not very creative to see meaningful returns. They don't hesitate to try new ideas to look at other ways. They are always open to suggestions and ideas. They lack creativeness enough to reap the rewards. This brings us to the other category, the Innovators. These are highly creative and take more risks as well. They are open to ideas and suggestions and they always try new things. They think outside the box; they always try to come up with new ways of doing things. New ways of promoting their books and breaking into the market. They often lack resources and guts to go for the big picture to become the leaders. They lack the financial backing to strike it big and often are afraid to go beyond the norm and form partnerships with the big players or borrow money to fund their projects. They are the future or tomorrow leaders; they just need the perfect opportunity to strike it big. They don't take much risks to strike it big instead they wait for a perfect opportunity to strike big. In some cases, they take their opportunities with both hands and strike it big but in some cases, they will wait for the perfect time which might never come. The difference between this group and the leaders is that, the Innovators normally wait for perfect opportunities to come. They keep an eye on their targets and wait. This is time wasting and in most cases the opportunities never arrives. The few authors from this group become leaders either by chance or they develop into big risks takers and big creative authors therefore becoming the leaders. These authors take the bull by the horns. They don't wait for perfect opportunities to arrive instead they create the perfect opportunities themselves. They form good partnerships with the big players and enjoy a part of the cake. They borrow money from the banks at low cost and invest this money.

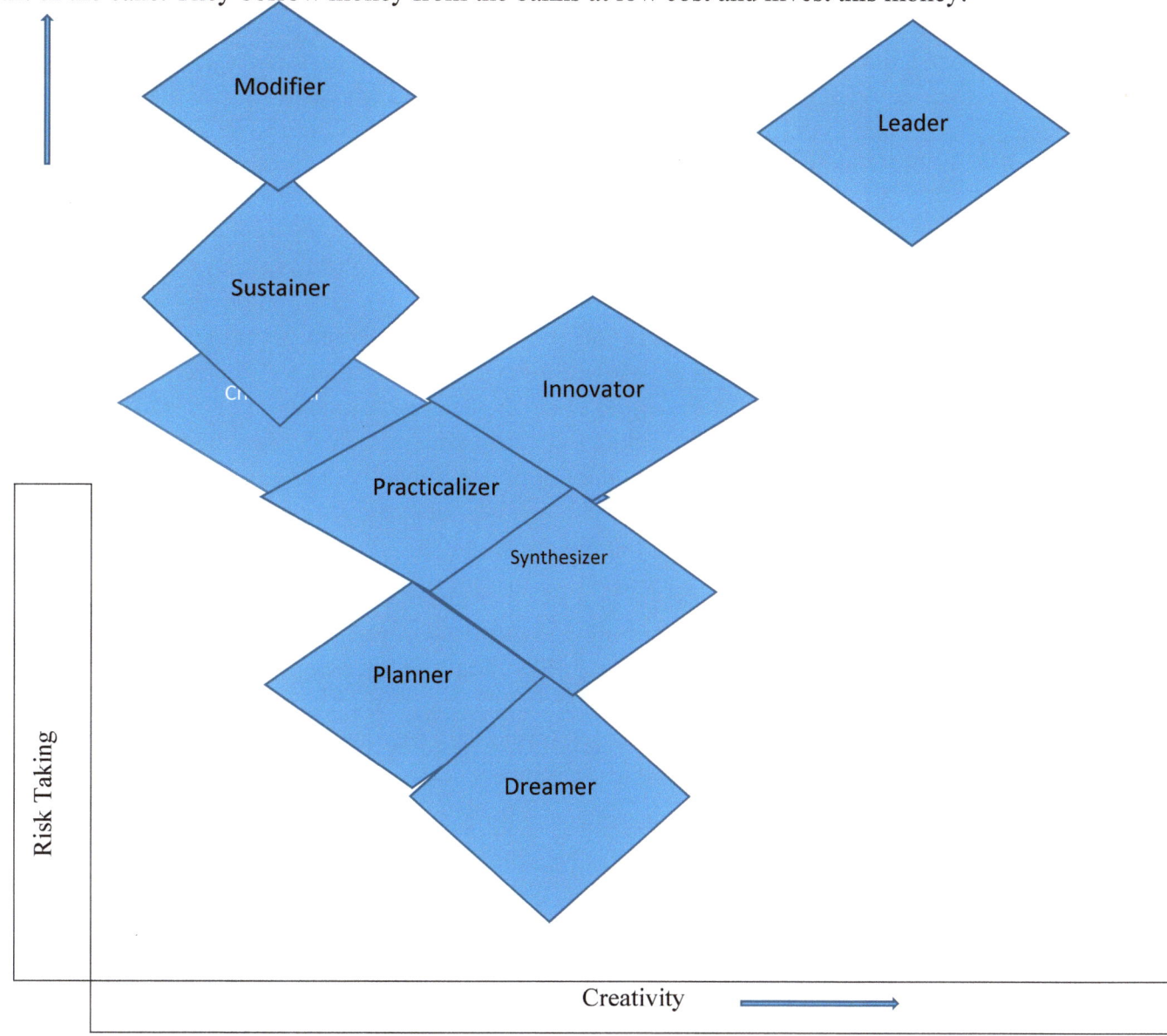

In other words, they are very creative, they look at ways of breaking the barrier. They look at ways of overcoming the current situation. They think outside the box and go that further mile to look for their capital and invest it when they are the leader. They are the head without the torso look at the diagram above. You will see it resembles a human body with a detached head. The headless body is where most authors fit. This brings me back to the point I made at the beginning of this book that to strike it big and rich one must detach themselves from the current situation. Get rid of the qualities associated with the rest of the categories namely the Innovators, the Challengers, the Practicalizer, the Synthesizers, the Modifiers, the Planners, the Dreamers and lastly the Sustainer. To strike it big you must think outside the box or body in this analogue. It's a complete distancing yourself from yourself, from your body. In short it's losing all your current practises and going further doing it alone. Think yourself as an own entity. You must provide everything yourself. You must write the book, publish it, financing it, promote it yourself to reap the rewards. All these big players they started as part of the headless torso going around in circles with no sense of direction. I remember some years ago when we went to our country house in the so-called village in Latvia. A chicken was taken from the chicken pan and beheaded ready to be cooked and somehow the chicken stood up and started running around. It was a disturbing scene as this was the first time I had seen a headless chicken running around. Likewise, people find it hard to make millions not become there is not enough money for everyone. The few who learn, understand and adapt these principles in this book are the ones who keep on becoming millionaires or billionaires. Sit down one day and start researching all the millionaires and the billionaires. Look at how they started their business and how and when they become big and rich. Most it's that understanding that you must distance yourself from your body. You must view yourself as the single entity the head and somehow you must find everything you need by yourself. To make real money you must think big. Most of these giants have started in the backyard garden, then they started to think big and viewing themselves as the head without the body. Somehow they just found a way of getting the torso they need, in the process expanding, thinking big and going globally.

I have dwelt more on the above ideas for you to better understand some of the methods, ideas and suggestions in this book. This information is like background material that will help you to understand some of the decisions I made later. First don't get me wrong I am not saying you can be a millionaire tomorrow or neither am I saying that today you cancel all your relationships and dealings with your publishers, no. I am saying this is the future, you can't achieve this in a day instead look at this as a plan you should accomplish in stages or phases. This brings me to the second part of the process to becoming a millionaire author.

Stages or phases you should take or make to become a millionaire author.

First sit down and look at the creatrix diagram above and honestly assess where you fit in as per today. Are you the Sustainer the Dreamer or the Planner. These authors write books and as soon as the book is complete their role is completed as well. They live everything to the publisher. They go with the flow the publisher dictates everything in the end they are there just to support the publishers grow big. They do little themselves to influence things. In the end, they will never make meaningful money.

Or maybe you are one of the Modifiers, Synthesizers or the Practicalizer you take part and get involved in the publishing and promoting process taking some risks and being creative as well. These are the better off publishers they have some influence in the whole process and therefore they reap extra income just because of their involvement. Nevertheless, they don't take enough risks nor are they creative enough to make a significant change.

Or maybe you are one of the top two groups the Challengers and the Innovators. These are the better offs authors they are very creative and they take risks. They make part decisions to the process of book publishing. They influence a lot of decisions in the whole process there by guaranteeing themselves big shares and rewards in turn. Like how I emphasized above these authors, they strive to be partners with the publishers and develop good relationships with everyone involved. They look at the big picture, they are starting to think big. They have realised at this stage that they must leave the headless torso and become the head themselves. They must distance themselves from themselves. In other words, they must abandon their current practises and methods and start to think big and independent. They are the head without the torso, therefore they have somehow managed to find a way of building the hand, the legs, the body that comprise the torso. They must find the capital needed to start their own business their own publishing company, they must form and maintain strong partnerships with the rest of the players. Once they have achieved this then they will be the leaders, the main players.

The ideal stages to self-establishing yourself as the leader in other words of establishing your own company to write books, publish them, promote them and distribute them. The true and only road to become a millionaire.

Stage one.

In this stage, you are the Sustainer and or Dreamer. You are new into the business of writing books. Probably this is your first book. You have no fan base or supporters you rely mostly on the publishing agents and companies to market and promote your book. You rarely set aside budgets for promoting your book. Normally in this stage your job ends when you have finished writing the book, you leave the rest for the publishing agent to take care of. The publishing company does everything for you have less creativity and you don't take any risks you have minimal or no influence at all in any decision making proses. You are there to sustain the development of the publisher with little or minimal rewards in terms of money. You have no bargaining power to influence any decision-making process. Even if you have some creativity you have no say or power in any way. This stage includes the Planners as well. Although one might want to argue that the planners should be in a different stage of development, they have little or no influence in any decision-making process. They have limited resources in terms of finance and negotiating powers. Don't get me wrong they draw plans and follow detailed methods but that's about it. Nothing seems to take off from the ground. The plans end up gathering dust in the garage or in the cupboards. With time, you will realize that maybe after writing your book 6 months down the line you are still in the same position with little money from the sale of the few books. It took you maybe 6 months to write the book and add more 6 months just waiting to hit the jackpot. You sit down and look at the sales figures and find out that you are still struggling, sales might have just started to take off but you are in no better position than 6 months ago. Here is where I come in.

First and foremost, I want to introduce you to this phrase that's common in engineering cycles but which I think can be adopted and adapted to writing and publishing circles. Imagine you are the owner of a land rich in minerals spread all over the area and as deep as 60 metres down that can be extracted. You have been extracting just a few minerals from the top and moving from area to area. You don't stay in one place for too long and you tend to move to other areas in the hope of coming back to the same area in the future to still extract some minerals. Although you are making money in the end you are failing to balance things. You have revenue but all your profits are being eaten away by the shear costs. You are not being profitable. You sit down and realize that maybe you need a new approach to this. Your younger sister comes in and said to you, "Big sister I am going for the swimming lessons and today I will be learning how to deep dive.", she takes her swimming costumes and left the house. You take your laptop and start to researching what is to deep dive hoping you might find answers to your problems. You realize that although you are extracting minerals from the ground you are only scrapping the surface before you move to the next area. You stop and start thinking about Deep Dive. You realize that this could be your answer. You are not making enough money to see meaningful profits. The gross profits you are currently making are enough to cover the cost leaving you with nothing or just little to go by. The same is true for most writers and authors and self-publishers. The big picture is to think big and go global but equally important is to think deep and big. It seems you are only taking the top layer although this is the rich part if it's a creamy cappuccino, you are leaving behind all the un tapped profits. You open your dictionary to check the meaning of the word deep dive; you find several meanings from brainstorming methods to methods of extracting data and to act of diving underwater to depth between 30-60 metres deep. You stop and think to yourself how is the term related to book publishing and becoming a millionaire. There is nowhere in the literature that it's a useful term to publishing books but I think it's an idea developed for brain storming and generating ideas that you can skilfully apply here to solve your problems and end that vicious circle that prohibits us to see the £millions of people take about. I will use this term Deep Dive loosely and explain as I go along.

One definition I found is that; *"Deep dive is a system to extract value from dark data."*

The other stipulated that; "Deep dive is a method to extract sophisticated relationship between entities."

The other definition reads that; "Deep dive is a trained system that uses machine to extract valuable data from a huge vast amount of unrelated data"

In recreational circles a deep dive can be a dive to depths below 30 metres as far as 60 metres under water.

In engineering and business circles this can refer to the strategic change accompanied by resource allocation and processes change from top down intervention.

At a glance, you will deduce from all the definitions and uses of the word Deep dive as to refer to deep extraction or analyses of information, situations, relationships, scenarios to understand causal-effect and relationship that can be used in decision making. From now on in this book whenever I mention the word or phrase Deep Dive I will be refereeing to the systematic collection of information about your readers, your market, your current publisher, the region or place you are selling your books, relationships and their forms between all players whether equal partners or subordinates. I will use this term or phrase to mean a guided and systematic penetration of the market extracting the interest of the customers before going to other areas or targeting different customers. I will use the term or phrase Deep dive to refer to the complete need to change or move away from the current practise to developing a complete new strategy that is supported by the allocation of resources and the intervention by yourself as the head.

Think about the analogue of the headless torso above. Whenever you here about the term deep dive it can also mean the detachment from you the head from your torso that is the current system. Lastly and not least I will use the term Deep dive to refer to the deep study or extraction of relationships between everyone concern and predict problems. In short I, will use the term whenever I think it's appropriate for readers to start thinking about digging deep and start thinking global.

In short although it sounds dodgy Deep dive should mean to target your book readers, get as much information about them what they want and provide books materials to satisfy them until you empty their pockets. That's my way of thinking nothing wrong with this, it's not like daylight robbery as my sister suggested the other day but this is satisfying the need providing books people want to read and books people will recommend to others in a flash and books people can do repeat sales on to give away as gifts to friends. The idea is to provide a total service from customer focus before purchase to aftersales. My sister came to me and said, "So your actual mean to deep your hands into the customer pockets and extracting everything until they are dry?". I stopped for a while, thinking, the first thing that came to my mind was hell no that sounds like stealing but then again I knew that this was legit and a morally correct method. You will be understanding your target audiences and customers for your book. Knowing their tastes and needs and then provide books with stories that satisfies that need. You will be understanding the problems they experience and try to provide solutions and answers. You will need time as well to respond to almost all of those who write to you either personally or through a dedicated hand. The idea is to comprehensively satisfy the target market once they are satisfied you can move to the next target group and area. The idea is to extract what you can within a short period and move to the other area with little or no hope of returning to find new customers. In short the idea is comprehensively offer a book service to meet the needs of the target market. Have one good fictional book that you promote and make the audience relate to that book. Do all the customer service, sales and promotions and the personal parades or book signing tours. Try to sale as much as you can, encourage your readers to buy the same book to give to others as presents. Discourage sharing of the book, put more efforts in book design so it is not cheap enough just to give away. I was once given a book as a gift when I was a child. The book was beautifully designed that I valued the book and refused to share it with others and when I shared it with others I made sure that no one put marks on it. Understand the target customers and try to be creative and incorporate some things they might like that can be sentimental to them. Whatever it is Deep dive for information.

Most of the stuff I wrote about above might be new to you in the sense that you still in stage one of the development process although you have heard about this you have never practised it. Most authors at this point they leave everything to the publisher. Most publisher provide mass promotions, mass advertising and mass aftersales support. Ok so how can I move up the ladder and go to stage two.

Ok I reiterate the points above.

Deep dive to extract as much information as you can about your target customers, your relationship with everyone concerned, the region, cultural and geographic factors that can either make or break your book campaign and sales. This is the key attribute most people in this stage don't have. The ability to Deep dive and understand the needs of their market. And because they haven't Deep dived they cannot be as creative as they can. Creativity is a baby of abundant information that can be easily Deep dived. You are new to the scene; you don't know anything how can you be creative? How can you take risks? Therefore, how can you be successful? Remember at the beginning of this book I wrote that success is influenced by amount of creativeness and the ability to take risks. This is true, Innovators have creativity but without taking the risk they might not realize their dream of becoming successful millionaires. This is true, look at all these inventors most had their ideas developed after they had died. They took years to take that risk to put their ideas into action. They lacked the insight to assess the risks of taking certain steps needed for them to achieve their dreams. They had the ideas and they waited for the perfect time to arrive so that they can implement their ideas and unfortunately that perfect time never materialized. Why? Because they were not brave enough to take the risk of getting funds somehow to test their ideas. Look at those who are successful today. Most they only developed someone's idea and they took the big risks of funding the project somehow be it through a bank loan or a partnership deal. They showed the guts and didn't wait for the perfect time to arrive but instead they went searching for the perfect time. They say fortune favours the brave. That is true. Those who are creative and risk takers are often the most successful ones. Now then, the authors in this group have little or no risk taking or creativity behaviour.

The answers are for them first to Deep dive. Understanding who you are dealing with. Try to link the patterns you can observe. Look for causal-effect, look for related links, find a way of making audience fall in love with your work. Make them personally attach to you and your work for you to be able to extract the maximum you can within a short period. Satisfying a need and making your audience commit and make repeat purchases of your books to give away as presents.

Secondly use the Deep dived extracted information to integrate some ideas customs and habits associated with your audience to be part of your promotional campaign. A good example is the use of small sentimental symbols or jewellery that is not very expensive to be sold as part of your book these can act as page holders etc. In other words, start thinking Deep dive as getting deep into their pockets and then start think globally. Satisfy your target audience before moving to another area or category. Listen to the idea, think big, think deep and think global.

Don't do like what most authors do, sticking to one category either mystery or science fiction. Look again at that diagram above about the different levels an author can be depending on their risk-taking behaviour and their ability to be creative. You are part of the headless torso; you are like a headless chicken. You need some guidance you need to escape, follow your head. You are part of the torso. Say hell No! I want to swap positions I want to be the head. I want to jump out of the torso. Look again at the diagram above the head is not on the torso or anywhere near the torso. Why? The head think big; the head think deep the head think global. But the head need the torso to function properly. The torso has weak legs in the form of the Sustainer and the Dreamers who are neither risk takers nor very creative. Theses slows down everything. If the head is to remain with the body, there will be less achievement. The head must operate the body away from the body. In layman's terms to succeed move away from yourself, dig a small hole and spit in it say I want great things I must completely change. Start moving away from yourself. Start changing, do everything differently. Copy the head. The head is the leader because the head thinks different. The head is in its own category. Look at the diagram again the head (leader) is above the torso and far to the right. The head is above and beyond everyone (the torso). To be a millionaire selling books unless you are one of the few who just write one book and make it big, you must write another book target a different audience. This part of start thinking global, start thinking big. You have Deep dived, to be big you must satisfy different or many customers. The globe is full of different taste, people, likes, needs and wants. You can either start a series pack to ensure commitment and attachment to yourself or you can target a different category. Start thinking like that. Look at the head the leader most they end up selling different things than what they originally started with. This is a good example of deep dive. You must keep on satisfying the same people providing all they want and need there by extracting value from them as well. Deep dive into their pockets, meet the need and get the money short and to the point.

It's all related. Start thinking big, start thinking deep dive as in extracting feelings and knowing their wants and needs and start meeting the needs. In turn start thinking about deep diving into their pockets, and finally start thinking global. This in turn will activate the need to be creative and therefore allows you to take risks to meet that demand. Most authors today don't think about deep dive as reaching deep into their target customers pockets. Most assume selling a book is all they must do, so would you be surprised if they can't make millions? I am giving you tried and trusted ideas that work. I might have other factors that are prohibiting me to realize my full potential but you could be better off. I am young only 23 years of age and I might not get a loan that you can easily access. You might have savings all your life which I don't have. Look at all successful authors, business, companies etc. They all have spent hours if not sleepless nights thinking of best ways to jump into their target audience's pockets and extracting everything until they are dry.

Look most successful authors they sell something else to the customers who buy their books. They have deep dived and extracted information about what their audience want, or need and their daily habits. Look everyone sell something else in partnerships with others. Some sell flowers with their books, some sell emblems as book holder or incorporates these as book covers. Some have discounted other products whenever one purchased a book. They have linked books to music and films. They have linked books to entertainment as well. I remember years ago when I was still a school there was an advert in which a gun was offered at reduced prize to anyone who bought a book. I thought that was the weirdest combination or complimentary items to sell together but this is a severe form of Deep dive which is to deep down into their pockets and extract their money either way.

In short understand your audience needs and wants look at the whole picture, look at the big picture start thinking big start thinking global. Distance away from your own torso, from yourself, you are the reason why you are not making millions. Stop thinking like you the torso but start thinking like the head, your leader and start following his or her shoes. Look at what the leader has done, how he has achieved that and say I am the head, I am the leader and on a small scale imitate the leader. The leader has imitated someone else. Most of the best business ideas have been around for thousands of years to be honest but they have evolved over the years with generation after generation after generation adopting these and modifying them. These methods have been tried and trusted and proven to work. Don't waste time thinking of a super idea. Read the small print and understand that the leader your head is in a better position today because she or he thought big, she or he thought deep dive as in extracting at one place until it's dry and then she or he has thought global. Walmart started as a corner shop then thought big, then Deep dive and then went global. Amazon good example too, spare room bookshop, then they thought big, they thought deep dive as in extracting and then they thought global. The only difference is that they were brave enough to search for the perfect time instead of you waiting for the perfect time to come to you. Stop today I tell you this. Run away from your torso, run away from yourself, distance yourself away from your torso meaning stop whatever you are doing. Start a new you. Start thinking different. Start looking for partnerships with all big players. Don't rely on anyone theoretically. Try to find your own solutions. Follow tried and trusted methods. Think big get out of your comfort zone.

I have adopted and adapted Deep Dive in the publishing circles to mean a complete strategic change in thinking, distance yourself away from your current daily practices. Start thinking big. Start thinking about funding your project, crowdfunding, loans, partnerships or using some of your savings. Start thinking like the leader, the head. This Deep Dive emphasize the top to down approach. Any meaningful intervention is from the top to down. Start thinking outside the box start making partnerships with other players. Look for alternative complementary food, things or products you can sell as part of your book. Have two or more books that target a different niche or market.

Launching yourself as the leader that means you start thinking big, start thinking Deep Dive and you start thinking global will not happen overtime but you can start planning now. I dwelt a lot above on this subject because all the methods and ideas I am going to use and show you have this notion as the cornerstone or the main theme.

Find ways of increasing creativity and awareness through Deep dive. Take guided risks at the beginning expanding due to experience gain. Effectively find ways of forming partnerships with everyone concerned. Start thinking about the future.

Now I am going to look at the ways to run your Amazon Kindle scout campaign which is the best way Amazon has given its readers a chance to be the head the leader. This is a rare opportunity to secure yourself a contract that is worth around $25000 in five years with an initial advance payment of $1500. Does that sound good enough? I think it's fabulous. Amazon has created a chance probably never seen before for you to run away from yourself, to leave the torso, to abandon your unproductive methods and empower all writers out there who have the guts to aim higher and go for glory. This is the best step towards making yourself a millionaire. Still you will need to observe and act upon all the ideas and advise given above to make it. It sounds hard but I personally think it is achievable.

What is the Amazon Kindle Scout Program?

https://kindlescout.amazon.com/

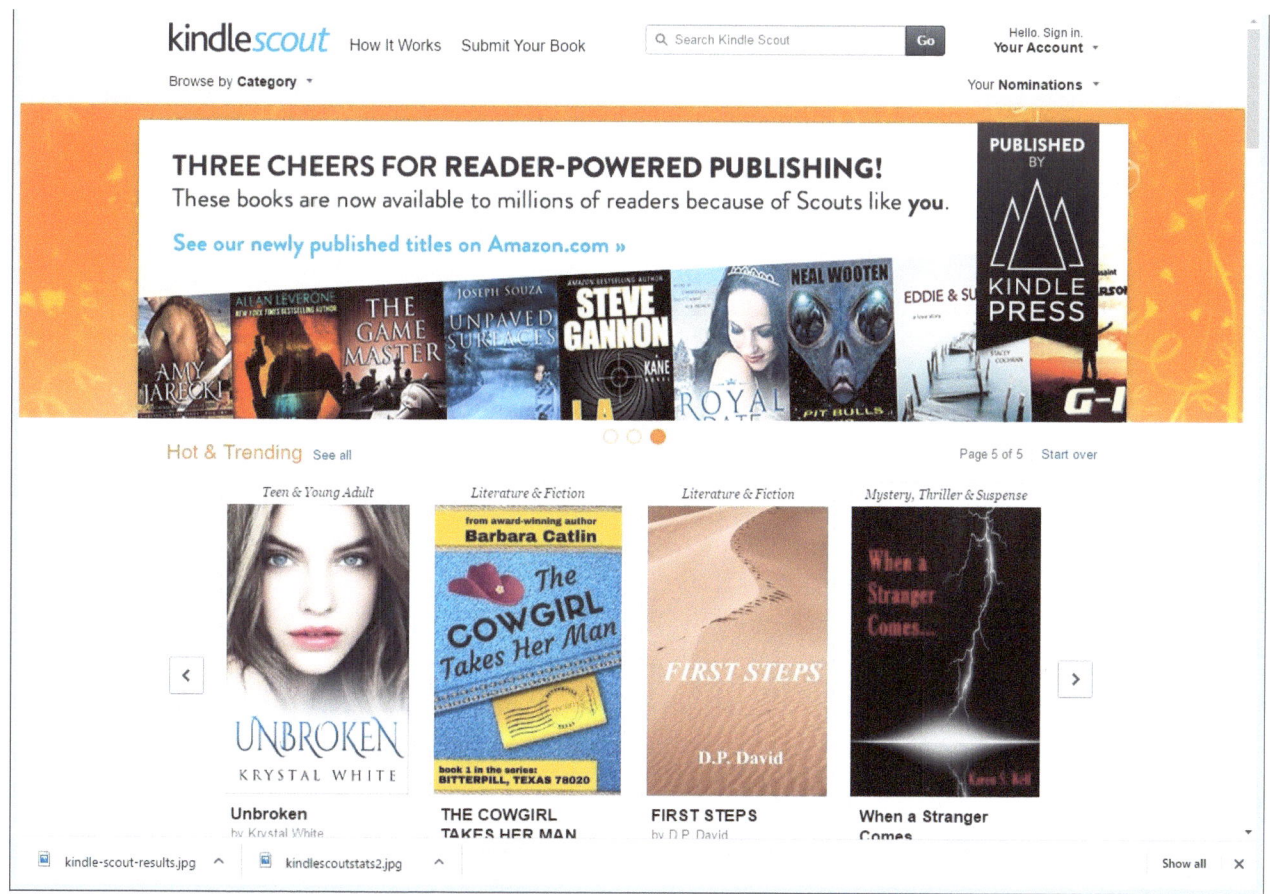

kindlescout.amazon.com/p/1N5BYLN9OGELY

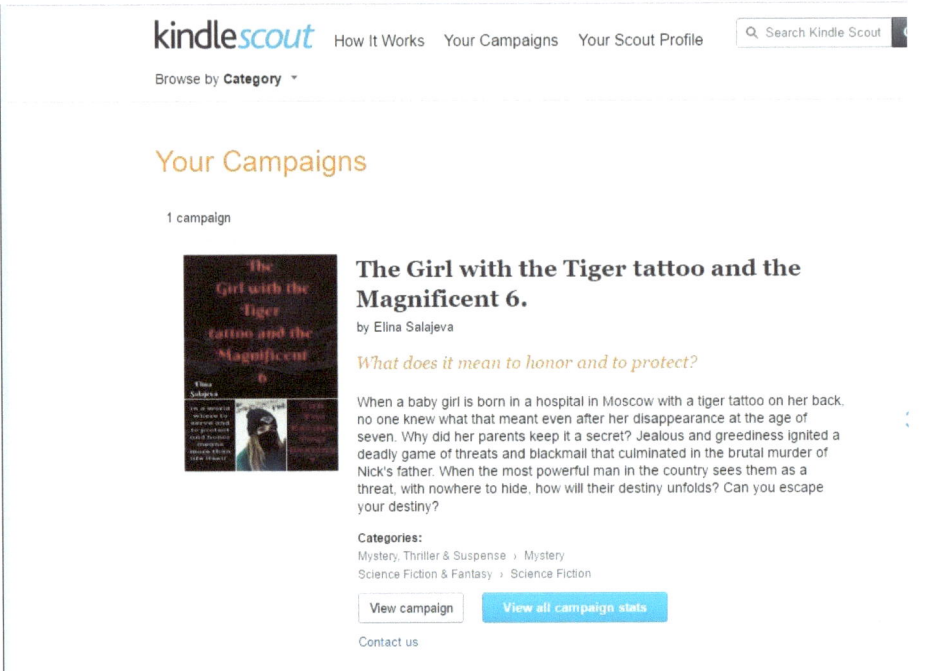

Per Amazon's Kindle Scout website this is the platform they have laid down as a way of empowering the authors to have a publishing contract in less than 45 days if they publish never written before books. Readers here have a say in whether the book gets published or not.

As the author, you will submit your book following the guidelines provided. You will also be asked to read and sign the publishing and submission guidelines and depending on how busy they are within two working days you will be notified of the campaign start date. You will be given a preview link to your book to review and after that the book will be launched. From now it will be your campaign that will determine to some extend whether you will be given a contract or not. The link to your book on the Kindle Scout website will be sent to you via email. After the launch date, you will have 30days to campaign and request for nominations. This is the challenging thirty days of this part probably one of the best experiences you will have. The camping is one roller coaster and believe you me it takes more than just sending emails and business cards. This is the part I come in. I have gone through this and I can happily say that I have learnt a lot of stuff, a lot of Dos and Don'ts. I have gone my way to try and understand the reasons behind this and the best methods to effectively run the Kindle Scout campaign. I have used methods I have learnt somewhere else, in fields not related to publish but with some very positive insights.

Remember the diagram above the one we talked about in detail about the Sustainer, the Dreamers, the Planners, the Modifiers, the Synthesizers, the Practicalizer, the Challengers, the Innovators and the Leaders. Yes? Amazon has given us the chance to move away from the Synthesizers, the Dreamers and the Planner towards the Innovators and the Challengers. If you are new to this publishing arena you will experience some problems but don't be shy or worried about this I got you covered. There are a lot of factors which you will need to considered to see which method is best for you. If this is your first time on the publishing scene you will have a lot of work to do.

If it's your first time to the publishing scene here is your tried and trusted guideline to effectively running the 30-day campaign challenge with the aim of securing a lucrative contract worth £25 000 in five years.

Step 1

Clearly define your goals, be assertive, know exactly what you want and be determined to achieve that.

It's all about planning ahead effectively set up your goals and clearly define what you want to achieve and how you are going to achieve that. The goal here is to attract potential customers and divert these to your website encouraging them to nominate your book.

Step 2

Get all the resources needed, if you are knowing and this is your first time to write a book, you must be very fast. Organise and plan well ahead. Open all social network account. Open Facebook account or page with the title of your book. If you don't have a personal account on Facebook open that too. Open a twitter account. Open a LinkedIn account in your name. Open a Tumblr account. These are the main social network accounts you will need to successfully run your campaign. There are other social networks you can join and create an account like Myspace, Youtube, Okru, Weibo, WeRead, Branchout etc.

Target your audience know your customers or potential book buyers and specifically target those ones. Main idea is to target those familiar with the Amazon Kindle Scout, and everyone who has a kindle author or reader account and all potential people you can bring to Amazon kindle. The idea is to leave a mark at the beginning of the campaign so after opening your twitter account. Don't just follower everyone or those they recommend to you. You know what you what *see step 1 so choose* only to follow groups or people related to or with something to do with KDP or Amazon kindle books. The reason being that for someone to nominate you they must have a kindle account. Don't waste time targeting the celebrities and all that stuff. You need people who have the time people who will bother nominating your book. This is the mistake most people make. Unless if you already have a sound fan base, you must be very selective in choosing who to follow and who will nominate your book. Remember after several people you follow twitter will automatically inactivate your ability to follow others. You will need at least 5000 people you followers for you to be able to gather enough people who will support you. Establish common ground when choosing followers. Common interest, in this case it's book writing, kindle, amazon kindle Scout, kindle readers, promoting your books, etc. I would encourage you to follow KDP Amazon first on twitter. Deep Dive as in the previous chapters, try to extract as many people you follow from there. This is the rich hub of all potential future supporters with nearly 29K supporters.

Deep your hand in there and if you can grab as many as you can minimum maybe 1k. These people are in the same shoes as you so that might give you a hand in the future. You are writing a book to sell in the future so start gathering a fan base. Follower Kindle Readers and extract as many as you can their follower as many as you can. You follower them and they will follower you too. If you are new, unless if you follow others it will be hard to quickly get followers. There are so many groups on twitter associated with Kindle book promotions. Followers most groups and from there you will win some followers. Ideally it is in your interest to name you accounts by the name of you book. Aim to follower a thousand people every two days if you can. So, by end of the first week you will have 2.5k to 5k people you follower and in turn you will notice that people will also start following you.

Do the same with Facebook. Open an account in your name and add a page or pages with the book title. Include all links you received in the email from the Kindle Scout Team. Don't just ask for friend requests from anyone. Back to step 1 clearly define your goals, know what you want to achieve and work towards achieving that. Target your audience you will have little time and resources so don't waste your precious time and resources. You need people or fans who will be interested in your book. You want to build a fan base. So, target your audience use the demography keys, the interest keys and other criteria like the region. Establish which countries are in the Amazon kindle program and include only these in the audience set up. No point includes countries that don't participate in the program because they won't be able to nominate your book. There are so many groups on Facebook join at least 20 by the end of the campaign. Aim to have a minimum of 500 friends who are kindle book readers and other authors by the end of the first week. Open a Tumblr account, a LinkedIn account, a youtube account, a Myspace account. Just follow the above guidelines and rules. Target your audience it's easy to just add anyone but when time comes will they be there for you?

Designing or how to arrange your twitter and Facebook profiles.

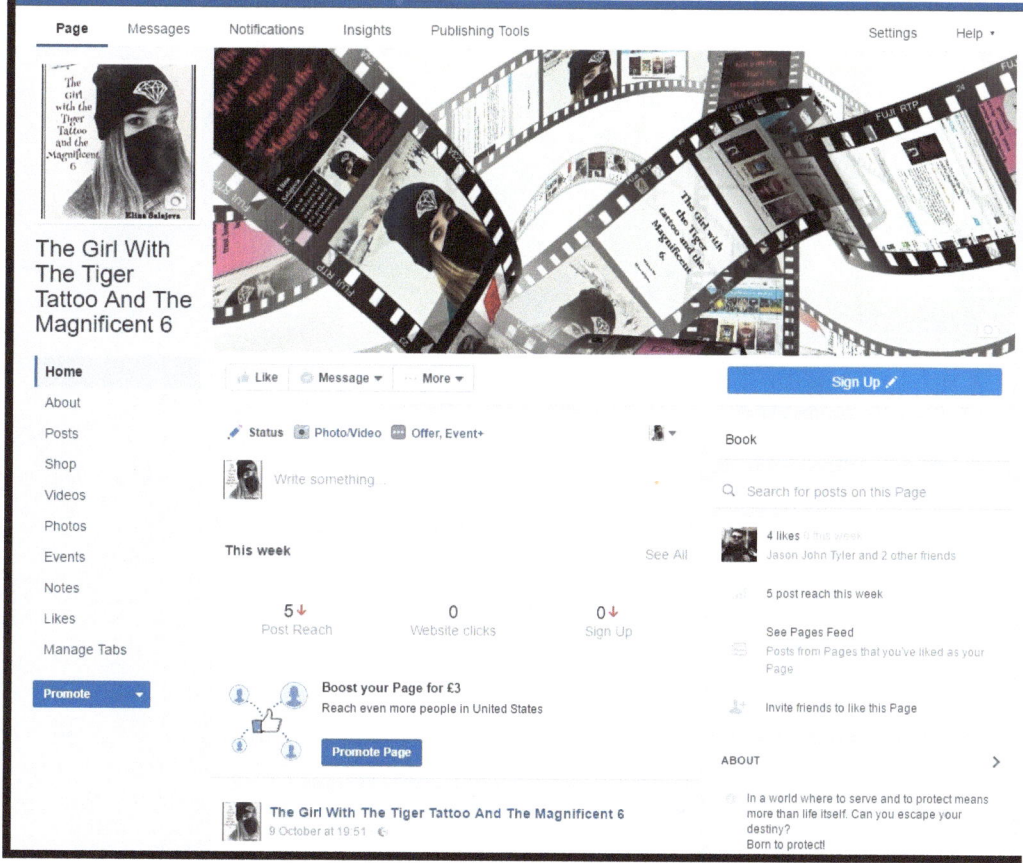

Be creative take a little risk try something new something different.

Make the website look professional, don't upload too many unnecessary photos or give too much information. Keep it simple and straight forward. You want people to get the idea of what you are trying to do a few moments after reading your website. Pin to top a post that explains why you need nominations and how the readers will gain by nominating you.

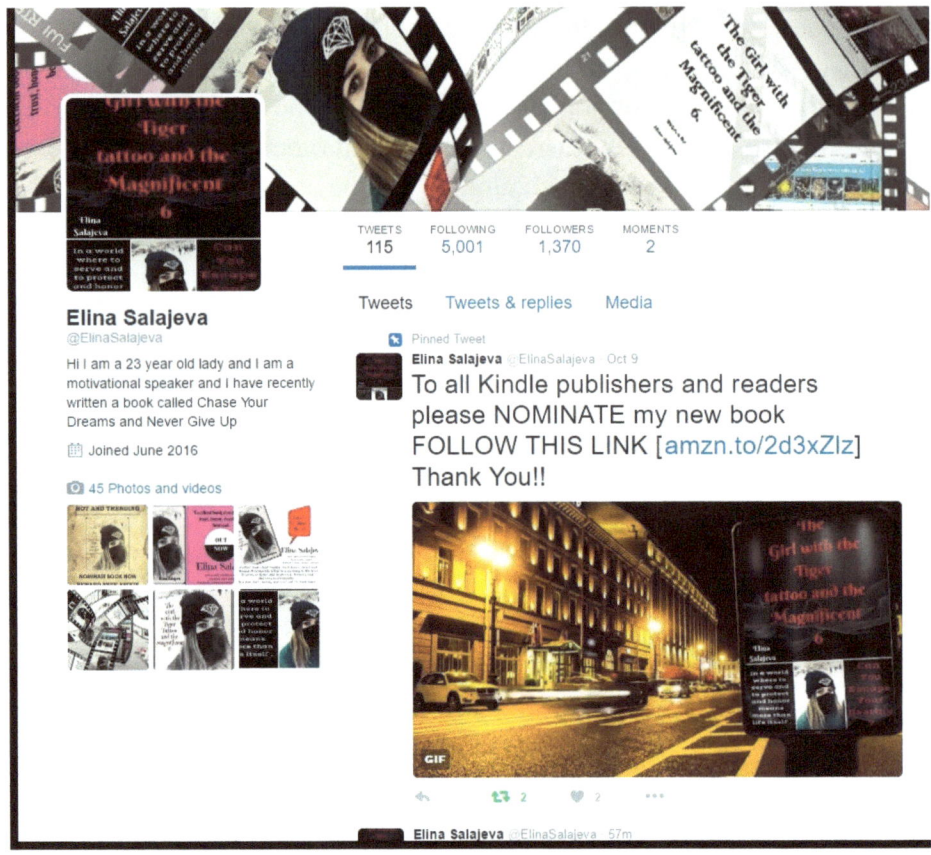

Sell your idea it's not financing gains they are after, it's the satisfaction they get after reading such a book. I have seen a lot of some author account. They seem all to form a similar pattern. Nothing wrong with that, remember what I said in the topics above. Run away from the torso, aim to be unique creative, fun, bring to the publishing arena things outside the publishing arena but things you like. Got stuck one day and I clicked you youtube, somehow there was that Bruno Mars video 24K. I Just twitted it and uploaded it on Facebook, since then a lot of people started visiting my profiles. People also started recommending my site to their friends. The bottom line is being creative, take a little bit of risk get out of your comfort zone, we are all humans, we like different things. Post a cooking recipe one day, a joke, etc. keep everyone interested attract more people.

Add the link to Amazon Kindle Scout on your profile, get a short cut free from the following website for you will need it.

www.tinyurl.com or from www.bitly.com

Add image of your book explain what the book is about and explain that you are on a 30day campaign challenge and you need everyone's help in nominating your book. Ask your friends to share your link and invite their friends as well. Use the *Invite friends function* on Facebook to introduce your website to your friends or potential supporters. The first week is to create a buzz, drive a lot people to your website, join groups and post your link into these groups. This is the fastest way of generating support.

Your tools you will need as set up. You now have a Facebook account, a twitter account, a Tumblr account, a LinkedIn account. There are other accounts you will need but for most you will easily get these once you have these four main ones.

The power of crowd speaking.

Your first of campaign has now just began. Congratulations you have opened your main social networking accounts but it does stop there.

Headtalker account.

Use your main four accounts, any one of the four to easy open a Headtalker account. This is the whole grail of campaigning. This is the new platform for crowd speaking. It's easy to create and start your campaign. Invite people to support your campaign. Go to Headtalker website https://headtalker.com/ And immediately start your campaign. Set a date just before your campaign ends say a day before your campaign ends so that your message will be share by those who have supported you. This is like grand scale advertising. On the day, your Headtalker ends your message will be shared by thousands if not million supporters.

Thunderclap account

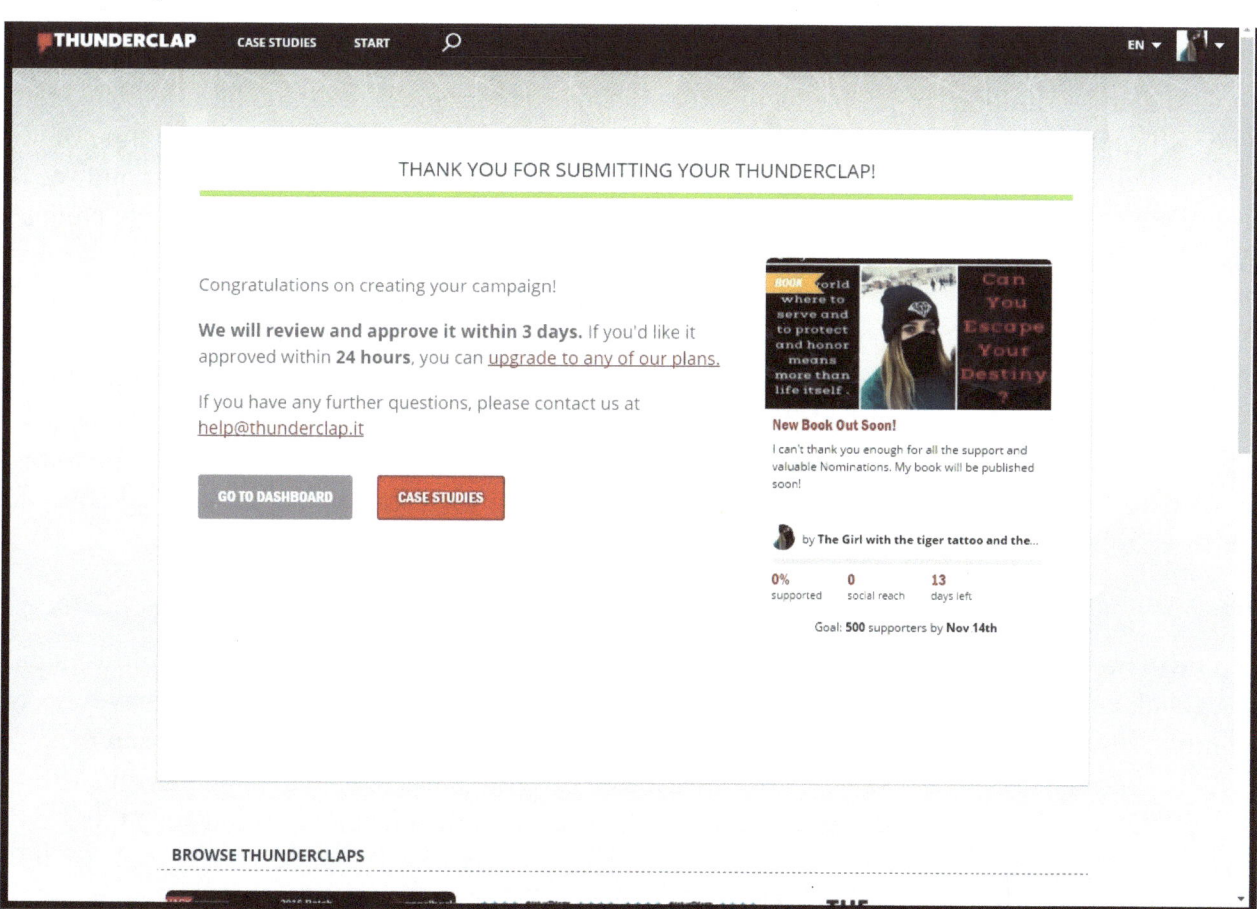

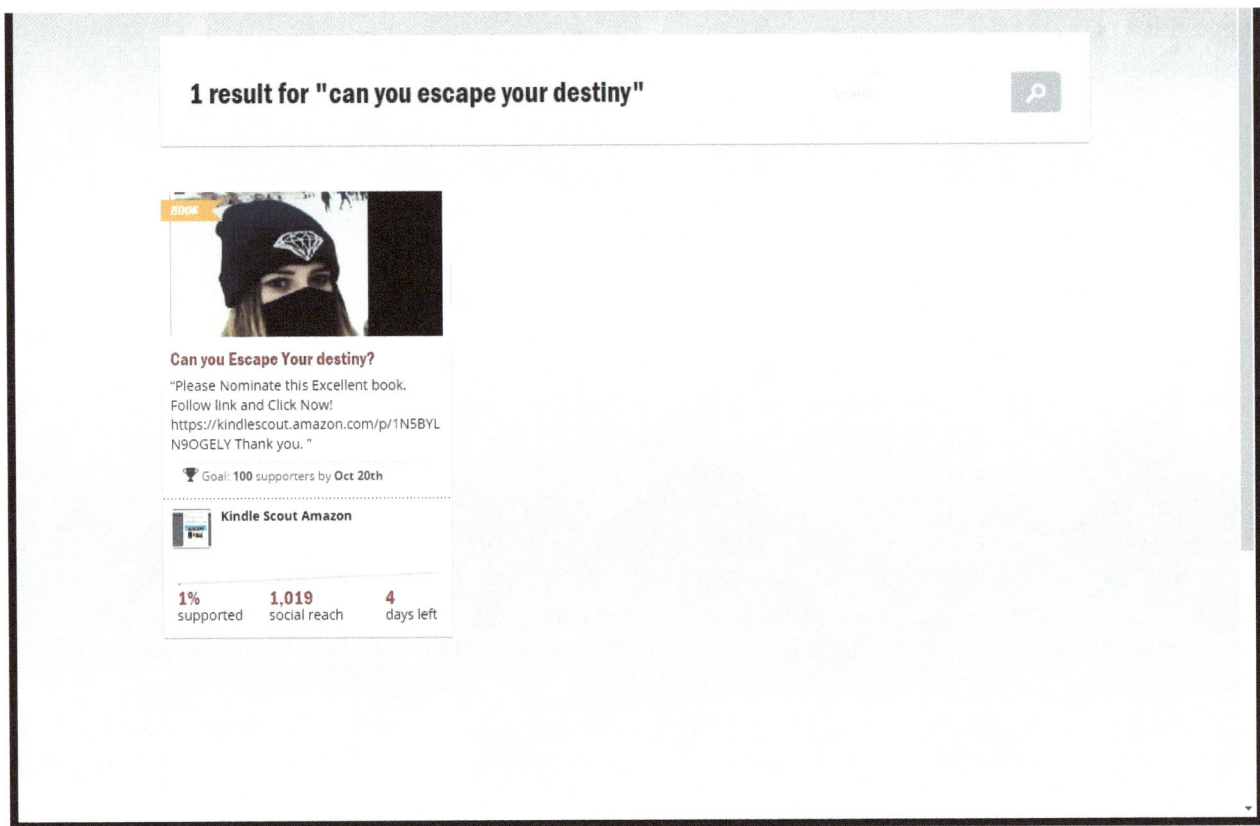

This is another social peaking platform with the aim of spreading your campaign message to thousand and or millions of people within a short time frame. This is the same like Headtalker, you will need a certain number of supporters for you campaign to be launched. At the time of writing you need at least 100 supporters to support your campaign. Set dates and times and wait. There are several methods that can be used and these will be looked at in depth in the chapters to follow. https://www.thunderclap.it/?locale=uk

Own website WordPress

Open a website free of charge use WordPress. You will have limited functions but trust me this will be enough you just need a website specifically designed for your own book. WordPress offers simply websites for free. Take advantage and link your account to this. Make the website easy to use and simple. Don't overload it with pictures. Just your front cover picture and possible extracts from your book.

Open youtube account

You will need to be creative somewhere down the line. Just image you have say 2k followers on Facebook and after the first week they will all have seen your message and most will have nominated your book by now. The second week you will still have the same fan base and they will have nominated your book already. Where will you find more people to support you/ After sometime everything will kind of stagnant. That's when you must be creative and keep the interest and the spirit high. You are not going to change the cover of your book, are you? So, try to be creative, think outside the box. Go a mile further, Deep dive understanding the people who are supporting you, extract information as much as you can. You will need to post a video or clip here and there. Make short videos to be different and to keep the interest alive. Aim to attract traffic to your Kindle Scout website.

There are other accounts you can join to spread the word of your campaign but so far these are the must have accounts.

Step 3

Budget planning. Would you leave things to chance or not?

The idea here is for you to be the leader, the head, this campaign is moulding you to that. Take control of things don't wait for chances to come knocking your door instead your go after all the chances there is. Facebook is a cheaper way of advertising and spreading the word of your campaign. They offer ways to boost your posts for as little as £3 per day. First week is crucial because you will need people to start nominating your book as soon as possible. Fist week aim to spend at least £21 that is £3x7days. Trust me this will be the best £21 you will spend in that week. You can either go the free-way too, I will explain this second method below. The assumptions here is that this is the first time you have done this; you have no fan base already you starting from scratch.

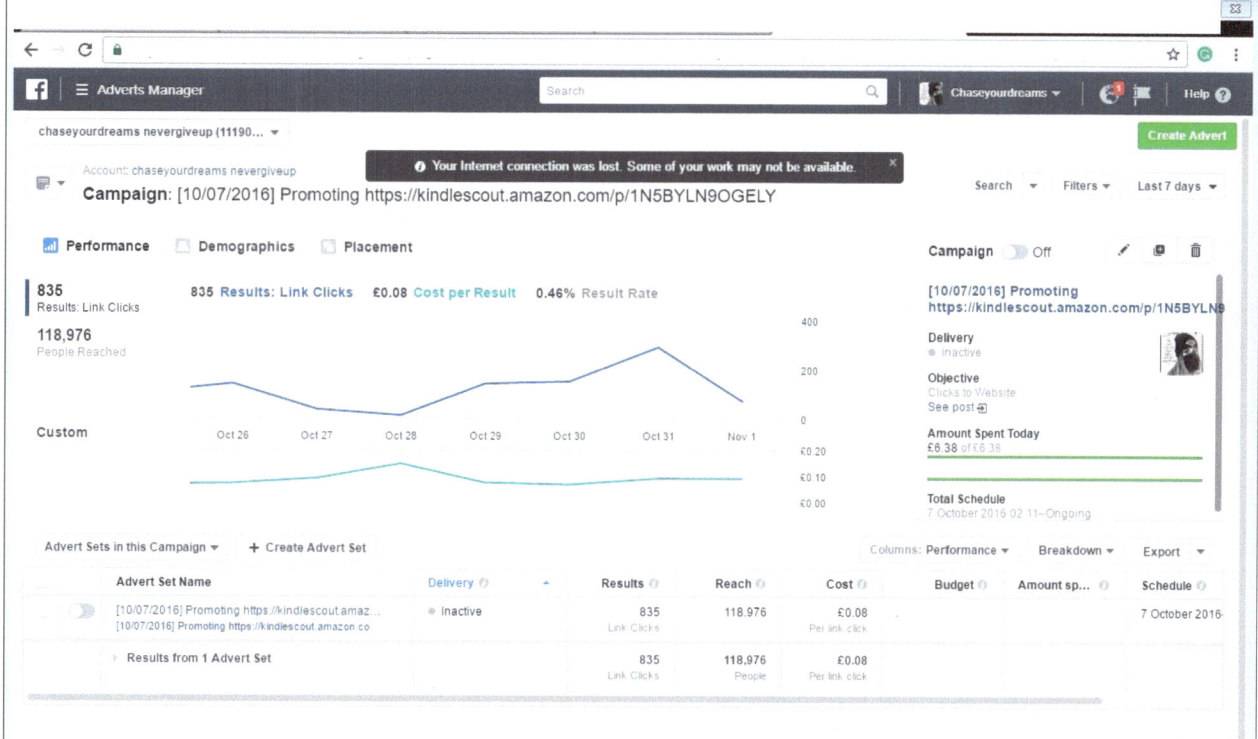

Above is my Facebook promotional campaign depending on your budget you will always get traffic to your Amazon site from Facebook if you are running an advert. The idea is not to leave everything to chance but to try and be in control and predict the outcome.

If you have a fan base already then the chapters below will apply to you. With face book depending on your budget you will be guaranteed Clicks and nominations of your book throughout your campaign. You cannot expect your fans to nominate your book all the time, I think it's one click per person and you will need at least 500 clicks per day to stay in hot and trending. For the whole campaign, it just depends on your circumstances some would benefit from spending £3 a day for the first week, or two weeks or the whole campaign. The idea is to set aside say £50 and need be then use the money to advertise on Facebook.

Step 4

People networking.

This should be done during the first week gather all those email address and make sure that your mailing list is up to date. Gather more email address and start your mailing campaign. This is vital too because this is more of a one to one communication and there are better chances that the people you email will respond to your requests. This is much better targeting with replies even greater than just posting a message to people you don't know. If you are new to the publishing forefront, then start gathering email contacts for you will need these.

Get your business cards designed cheaper they don't have to be perfect but they must have sent the correct message. They should have the name of the book you are promoting and the link they should click to nominate your book. You can get the flyers printed too and posters just depending on local circumstances.

Word of mouth is not very effective because most of these people have nothing to do with Amazon Kindle Scout. To nominate a book, you must have an Amazon Kindle Account. You can tell your friends and family but the returns in terms of nominations can be minimal because they lack accounts needed to nominate your book.

Step 5

It all start with Amazon so create an Amazon author central page.

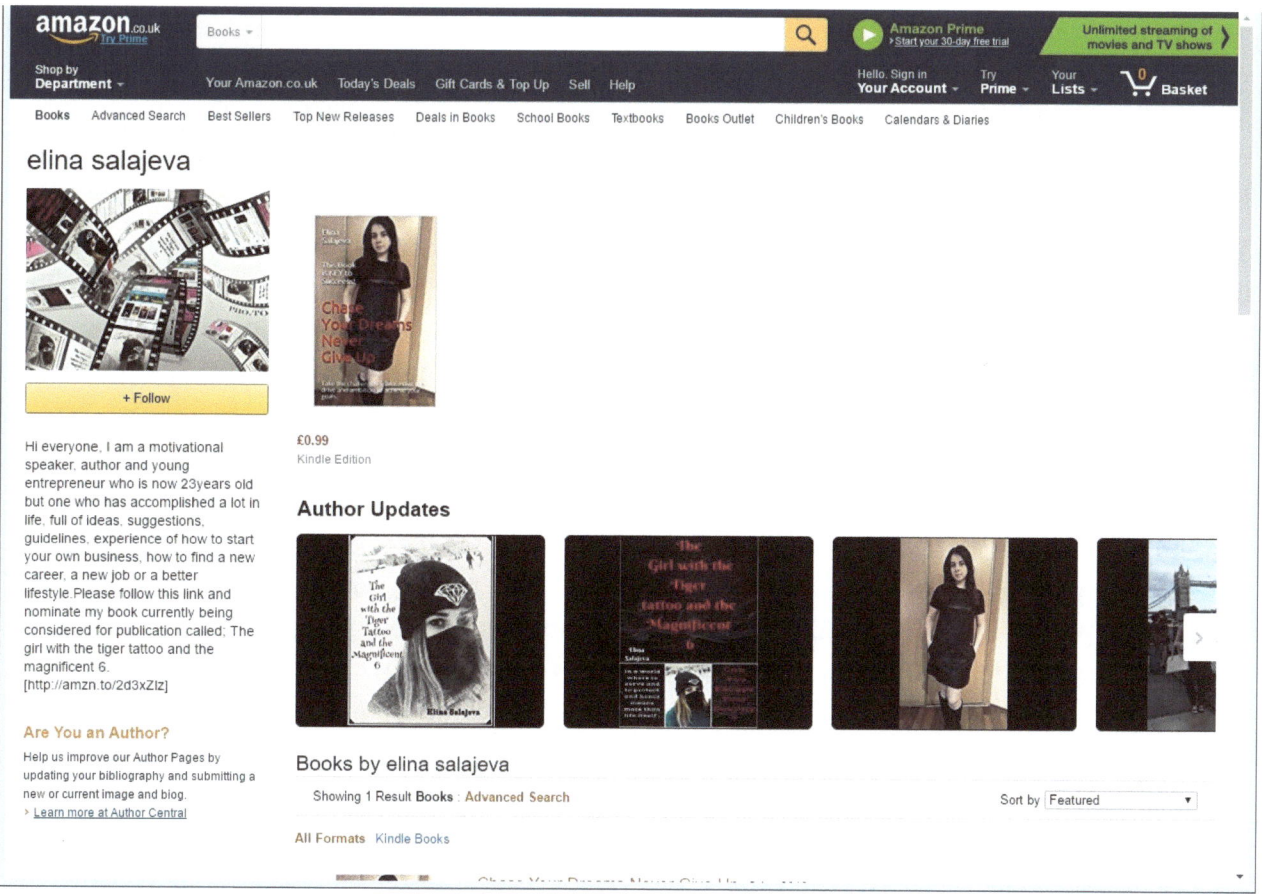

This is very important because people who will have much influence will be other authors and readers already associated with Amazon. There are hundreds of authors with Amazon author profiles. Connect with them share links ask them about their opinion as regarding your book. Follower them they will follow you back. This must be the starting point.

Step 6

Create a simple 30 second youtube video just to ask people to nominate your book the best short videos you can make can be done using this website www.biteable.com. The videos you make will have watermarks which you can remove for a small amount of money. These videos draw attention and arouse interest. They are simple make them very short less than a minute. Get two down one just to ask readers to click link and with a very big thank you at the end. The other video should tell the story of your book just as at the back cover of your book. Make sure you include links with the video descriptions. You can get a gif picture made that you can use to attract new visitor to your website.

Now that everything is in place you now have officially started your campaign. There are many methods people use or can use to approach this campaign. They all work different and the final decision rest with the Amazon publishers. From my experience and my research, I think I can say that there are many ways to kill a cat. First and foremost, ask your self-question in relation to step 1. What are you trying to achieve? You just want your book to be nominated and be granted that publishing contract. Correct? I think so. How you go about it is subjective there is no correct way or wrong way. I will first try to look at all the methods that can be employed to tackle this and then recommend one based on the information supplied.

Look at it this way. Assuming each of your fans and friends can only nominate your book once. In this case, it does matter whether they nominate your book at the beginning of the campaign or not, because that will not make any difference. The book will be in the campaign for the next 30 days so you have 30 days to run before the book can be considered for publishing. I will give you scenarios and then explain later own.

First let's assume that your fans and friends and any people you ask for nominations can only do that once. At the beginning of the campaign you have 200 supporters and they all cast their votes to nominate your book. And after that they won't be able to nominate your book. So, at the end of week one you have 200 nominations from everyone who has supported you. So, graph will peak to 200 page views. Come second week let's assume you did not get anymore supporters. In that case the graph will drop back to zero because in week two no one nominated your book because now they are not eligible. So, in this case you will have more people visiting your page in the first week and no visitors towards the end of the campaign where it matters the most.

The idea is to set a minimum number of people who will visit your page unless if you want to be on the computer for next 30 days. I would prefer the number of people visiting my page to grow every week as the news of the book spread. I wouldn't want a peak at the beginning of the campaign followed by a steady declined. By the time it's near the end of the campaign that's when I expect my book to be very popular and it will be valuable than to sell it to Amazon when it's interest is declining. This is subjective but an earlier campaign I saw on internet was exactly like I said above; a peak at the beginning of the campaign and a steady decline until the end of the campaign. I would think that it would be advantageous not to throw everything at the beginning but to save the best for last. So, having this in mind I would encourage you to compile a mailing list or twitter or Facebook contacts that you know you can use in week two or at the end of week one. First week would be ideally to have a major peak followed by an even greater peak in week two. The third week is probably the crucial one as the decision to give you a contract or not might depend on the results. The fourth week should be even better than the first weeks. The idea is to show that the demand for your book will grow depending on the amount of advertising and promotion you make. Ideally in a real world. First week your book will peak and drop a little bit as people are introduced to the book. In week two more and more people will be exposed to your promotional campaigns and the graph will peak too wee three should be the best week as you will have had the chance to promote your book and gather enough support. In week four the graph can rise even further which is good as you will want the campaign to end on a high note. They say save the best for last but is it always correct. This is subjective as we don't know how the publishers will make their decision. I personally think that it's not a good idea to exhaust all your efforts within the first weeks and end on a low note. I would prefer steady start but high peaks in week two, week three climaxing in week four. The method to adopt just depends with the circumstances and category of your book as well. If your book is in the category with little or no books you can still chance your book being selected.

I was just sat home watching an old program on television about the Elina's-Tsunami-Wave-Effect then it just clicked me. There and then, I just realised that that is what I wanted to see on my promotional graph. I thought for some time how I was going to achieve that. I read articles about Elina's-Tsunami-Wave-Effects and finally devised a way of emulating just that. This method of mine is called the Elina's-Tsunami-Wave-Effect effect.

The Elina's-Tsunami-Wave-Effect effect.

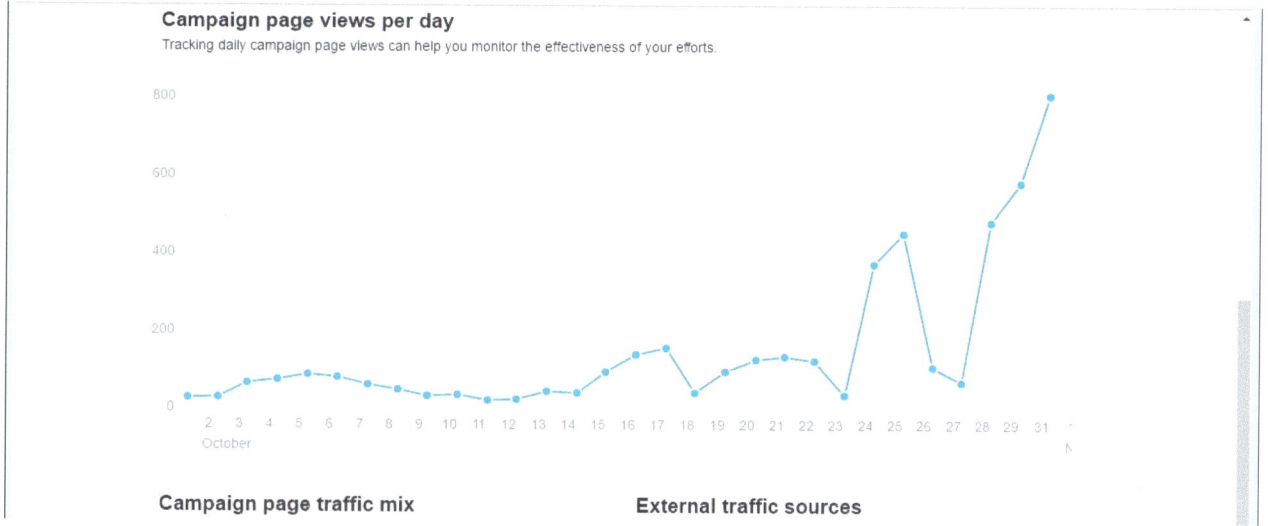

The above diagram is my KDP kindle Scout campaign graph. This is what I call the Elina's-Tsunami-Wave-Effect wave effect. The taffic to your Amazon website will gradually increase as you lay a solid foundation base. This is true in the first two weeks with the pressure building in week three eveident by a huge rise in page views per day. After establsihng a solid base and a huge loyal following as the news spread of your promotional campaign more and more people start talking about your book with the result of exponential increase in visitors to your Amazon page. The idea behind this is the need to establish a strong loyal fan base. The first weeks you have fewer page views because initially your main aim is to win these people. Let them associate themselves with your book, give them time to make their own decision once they agree to nominate your book and support you then they will be there fore ever. Like I said earlier on you need them to spread the word as well to help you build that fan base.

The idea behind this method is based on the fact that when the time comes for your book to be considered for publishing the buzz about your book should be at its heighest and not already declining. Over the first three weeks you were building a strong base, a very strong foundation that is unshakable. By week three you will start to see the benefits of your campaign. You will have established loyalty towards your book. Over the past three weeks people will have fallen in love with your book. The rise in week three is a s a result of your fans and potential buyers of your book spreading the news to their friends as well and the popularity of your book. I am assuming here that you had no prior fans and you started from scratch. If you were already established then this won't apply to you. The rise in page views in week three is as a result of your efforts and your fans spreading the news as well.

But if you are like me, you want always to hold the bull by its horns this will be a planned rise in page views. The question is how can one achieve that?

Here comes the Elina's-Tsunami-Wave-Effect effect.
Elina's-Tsunami-Wave-Effects are natural disasters associated with much destruction and enormous force. These are series of waves that gradually grow until the growing force produces enormous energies that sends the wave exponentially in the sky. With this method, you are guaranteed to see an exponential rise in page views from the third week until the very end of the campaign. The efforts from your campaign will gradually start to show at the end of week two. By week three you can see real major changes and by week four the page views will remain high. The book will have entered it's long and strong hot phase. Everyone will be talking about this book.
The advantages of this method are that whatever you are doing is building a strong fan base that is genuine and strong. Over the past weeks you will have been selling your ideas and promoting your book. By third week you will have gathered faithful supporters who will be there for a long time. This is not a quick and short lasting effect. Here your emphasis is on building the future audience, readers of your book whether you are granted the contract or not. The idea is not to generate a quick never lasting buzz in the first weeks and then struggle for page views at the end of the campaign. By the time Amazon reviews your book, your book will be more valuable that the first two weeks and if it was me I think I would buy or invest in a book like that than invest in a book that has already reached its maturity. Most people have the tendency of throwing everything the first two weeks and then struggle to promote and generate new people to nominate their book. With this method, you create a huge following and a big buzz just before the book is released which I think is good for sales. This is the best method as far as I am

concerned. You want to sell something that's hot something everyone is talking about. This is called perfect timing just before your book is published.

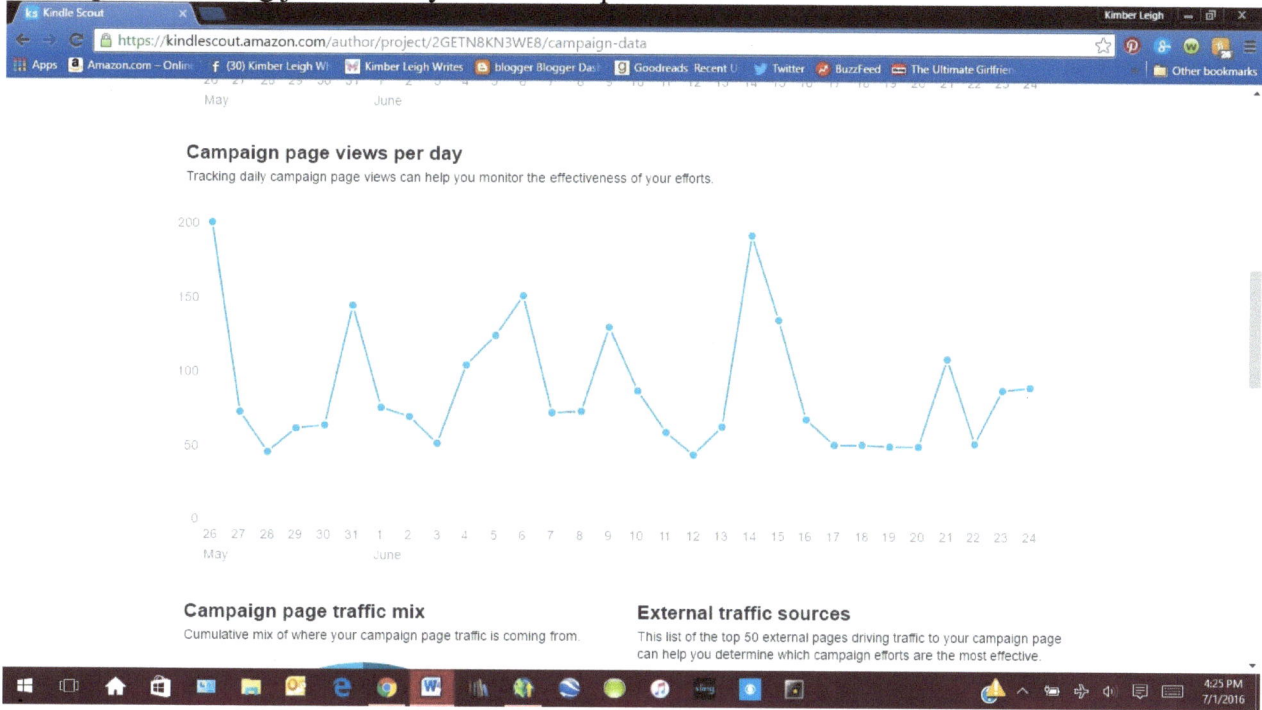

I will show you a good example of what I am talking about. Look at the graph below. This is probably what happened. I just found this graph on internet and guess what? The book was not accepted for publishing. From the above graph, you can tell that the person concerned probably threw everything in during the first weeks heating 200 page views first day and a deep to less than 50 the following days and picking again here and there but not as much as the first day. This is an example of lack of a strong fan base. This person probably just rushed to get nominations the first weeks and then struggle to even secure more than 100 the last week when I think your book should be rising in popularity and demand just before being released.

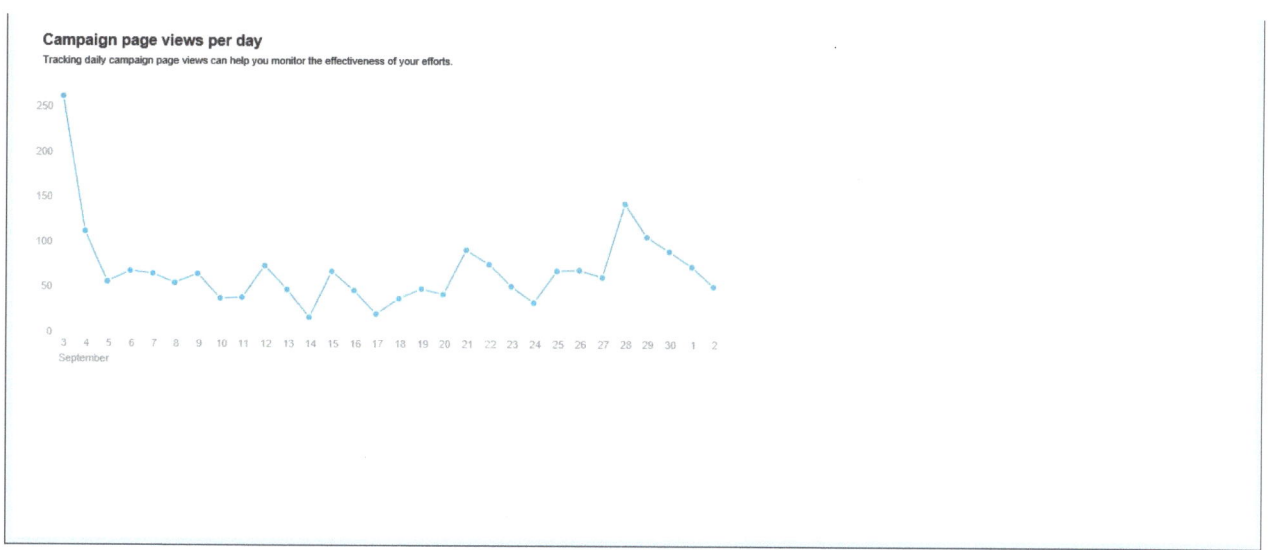

This is another example of poor planning and not understanding what is needed. Like the other person above they rushed into soliciting nominations without establishing a good sound foundation for their book and in the end the book was rejected too. You can see that there lack of understanding of the principles behind all this. You should thank me right now because at least you have insight of what is needed unlike the unlucky people above. Just imagine a cash advancement of £1500 straight to your bank and a lucrative contract worth £25 000 in five years surely everyone thinking about entering this Kindle Scout campaign would think twice and buy this book.

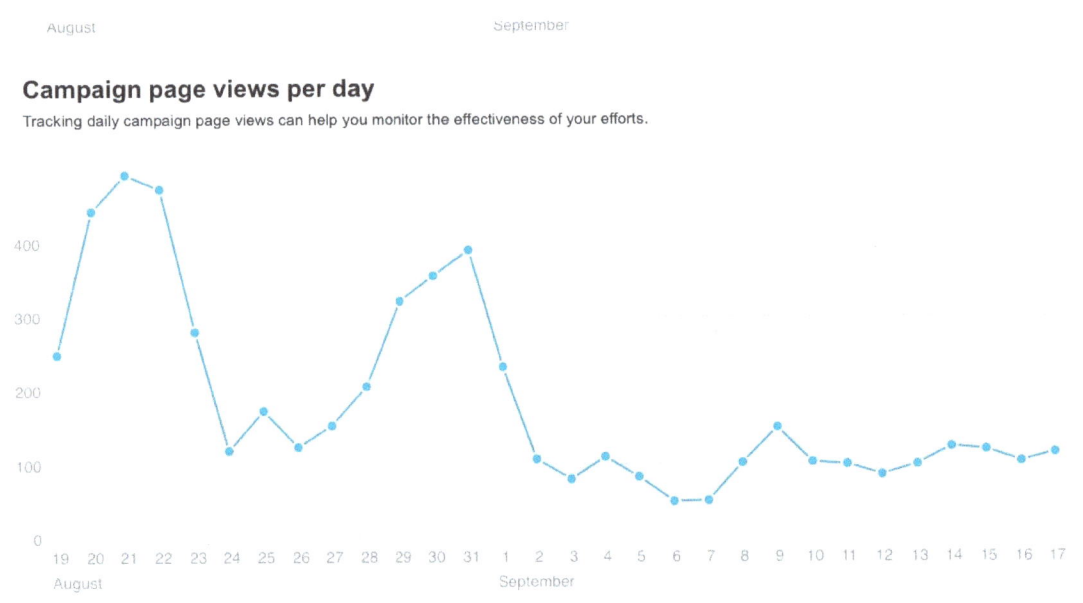

Campaign page views per day

Tracking daily campaign page views can help you monitor the effectiveness of your efforts.

Above is another failure, the method adopted is still the same with the devastating results. They say save the best for last and it seems to be true. Don't throw all your best soldiers in first when you know it's a long war you are fighting. Keep these until the end when you need them. The first weeks is for foundation building. Promote your book as if you are the head the leader, the publisher. Remember the idea of the headless torso above. This applies here. These people they are acting like the headless torso. Picture this campaign as a vineyard. You have grapes that you have just harvested would you straight away make wine and consume it? Or you would wait for the wine to be ripe and ready and then enjoy it. The idea here is to put yourself in the shoes of the publisher. You want returns on this book, right? So, you are looking at a five years' book deal if your book has reached its saturation or climax point in the first two weeks what's in it for me. I am looking to publish books that can last up to five years and still make me more money. If you are the owner of this book and you cannot lay a solid base, a good loyal following yourself then why would I give you a contract. Below is another classic example of failure because of lack of understanding do what is needed and what is required from you. The idea is for you to do your part. Show you can be a partner of the publishing contract so do your part establish the fan base yourself. Don't rush, plan everything clearly defines what you want to achieve and then work towards that. It's not easy as people think this is but this book will guide you through the whole process and provide the dos and don'ts and trusted working solutions and suggestions. The final decision is up to Amazon but I tell you this that if you follow the guidelines in this book you will be destined for glory.

Campaign page views per day

Tracking daily campaign page views can help you monitor the effectiveness of your efforts.

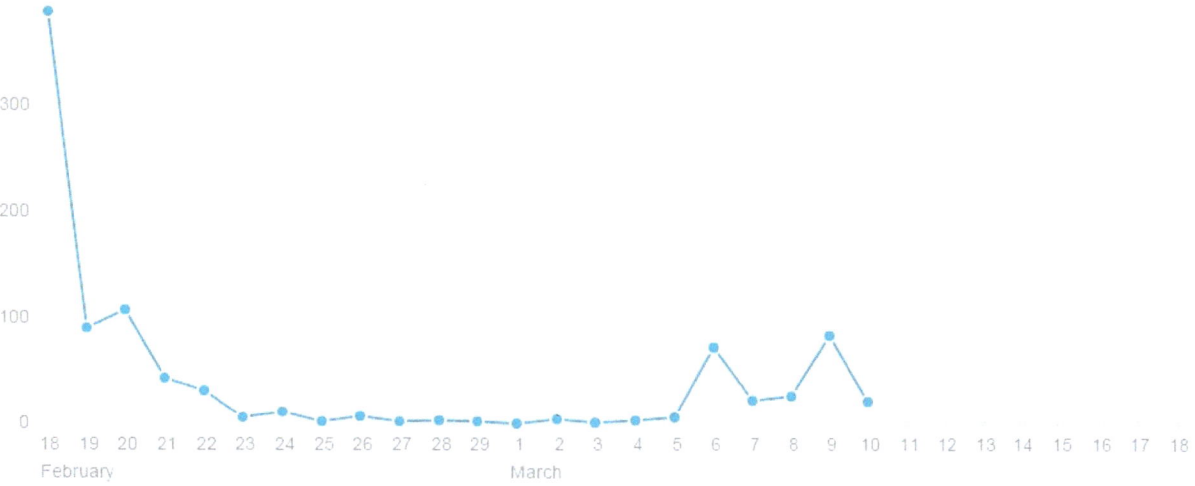

First and foremost, before I start explaining my Elina's-Tsunami-Wave-Effect wave effect there are things I think you should understand first and take into consideration. Look at the publishing contract again in other words they say read between the lines.

This is a five-year publishing contract. The idea is for you to think like you have 30 days to put real value to your book before you sale it at a premium to Amazon. So, having that in mind you do your work strive to establish a very strong foundation with loyal supporters, readers and fans. So, spend time building that up and laying the foundation. Second you want to make money as soon as the book is established so, try to make sure that when it's time to publish your book demand and the popularity of your book will be very high. Establish your book's website to show that you are serious about this publishing contract. There are a lot of website you can create for free. The best among Amazon Kindle Scout authors is WordPress because it's simple and free. It's easy to use and navigate and there are options to direct traffic to your website from there. Plan learn my methods in this book master them and then embark on you campaign. Having said that let's look at the Elina's-Tsunami-Wave-Effect wave effect.

Elina's-Tsunami-Wave-Effect wave effects method

The idea behind this method is that initially you want to build a strong fan or supporters base that will gradually grow during the first weeks and exponentially explode during the end of the campaign. The idea here is to establish loyal support who in turn will be vehicles for spreading the information to their friends and others. The idea is to inform potential supports about your campaign, your book and everything else.

Rule number 1

Don't rush to ask for nominations the first few days but try to gather support give the people chance to read your campaign page view and familiarize with your book. Let them make their own decision without you pestering them for nominations and support. Introduce them to yourself your book and explain the campaign first. Tell them this is once in a life time opportunities to change your life. Explain you need this and equally sell the book. You are not looking for favours but for them to like your book to fall in love with your book. Show that you don't just want nominations but you want them to be part of not just this campaign but for the future. Give them time tell them you are not pressuring them for nominations but you will check on them again after two days to get a general feedback about what they think about the book. Give them at least two days to look at your book and make up their minds. In the meantime, promote your book to others try and find new supporters. There are other people who can't be bothered but nevertheless who will just nominate your book and there are plenty of them in the first weeks. That could explain the initially peaks, once these have been exhausted and are no longer to vote you will see the curve going down again. This will be time to go back to those you initially asked to look at your book and get the general view about what they think about your book and ask them if you can count on them when you need support.

The idea is to try and join new related groups the first weeks and post in the groups rather than soliciting for support individually. You will notice that most people tend to ask from individuals the first weeks which is counterproductive. You are looking at real growth in number of supporters after week one so join these groups and post in that group using the share function on Facebook or post directly on their twitter page. With posting into groups you will find that you will huge responses after sometimes. Some groups will "study or review" your book in their group which is good. You need genuine supporters, people you will count on. These people when they are satisfied themselves they will spread the news on your behalf.

Keep the interest alive be very creative and take risks, approach other authors ask them for their opinion and ask them to review the first chapter on Amazon page. Get them to give you feedback if they can. Not everyone will agree but this is the game. Create something new every week. Change picture cover on your website, introduce a very short video www.biteable.com. Drop a latest song from youtube twit parts of your books to generate interest. Don't ask for nominations every day from the same people plan everything there are a lot of groups out there especially on twitter and Facebook.

After that has been done in the first 2-3 days you must plan the initial wave.

How to plan the Initial Elina's-Tsunami-Wave-Effect wave.

This is the first thing you should do. First day or two after joining the two-crowd peaking platform Headtalker and Thunderclap plan your Elina's-Tsunami-Wave-Effect waves. You will need at least three small campaigns using Headtalker and the big Elina's-Tsunami-Wave-Effect will be provided by the Thunderclap campaign. This is because Thunderclap is for big crowd speaking platforms as they require a minimum of 100 supporters. This is usually for big national or multinational campaigns as it is not easy to get 100 supporters. If you don't get the 100 supporters, then that means that they won't send your messages. Whereas with the Headtalker campaigns you will only need a minimum of 25 supporters and they are usual a lot of people who will support you without even asking them, The Headtalker has a lot of groups on Facebook and twitter and it's their duty I guess to support anyone taking part and using them to promote their books or something else. So, having said that let's look at the first wave.

Initial Elina's-Tsunami-Wave-Effect wave using Headtalker as your crowd speaking platform.

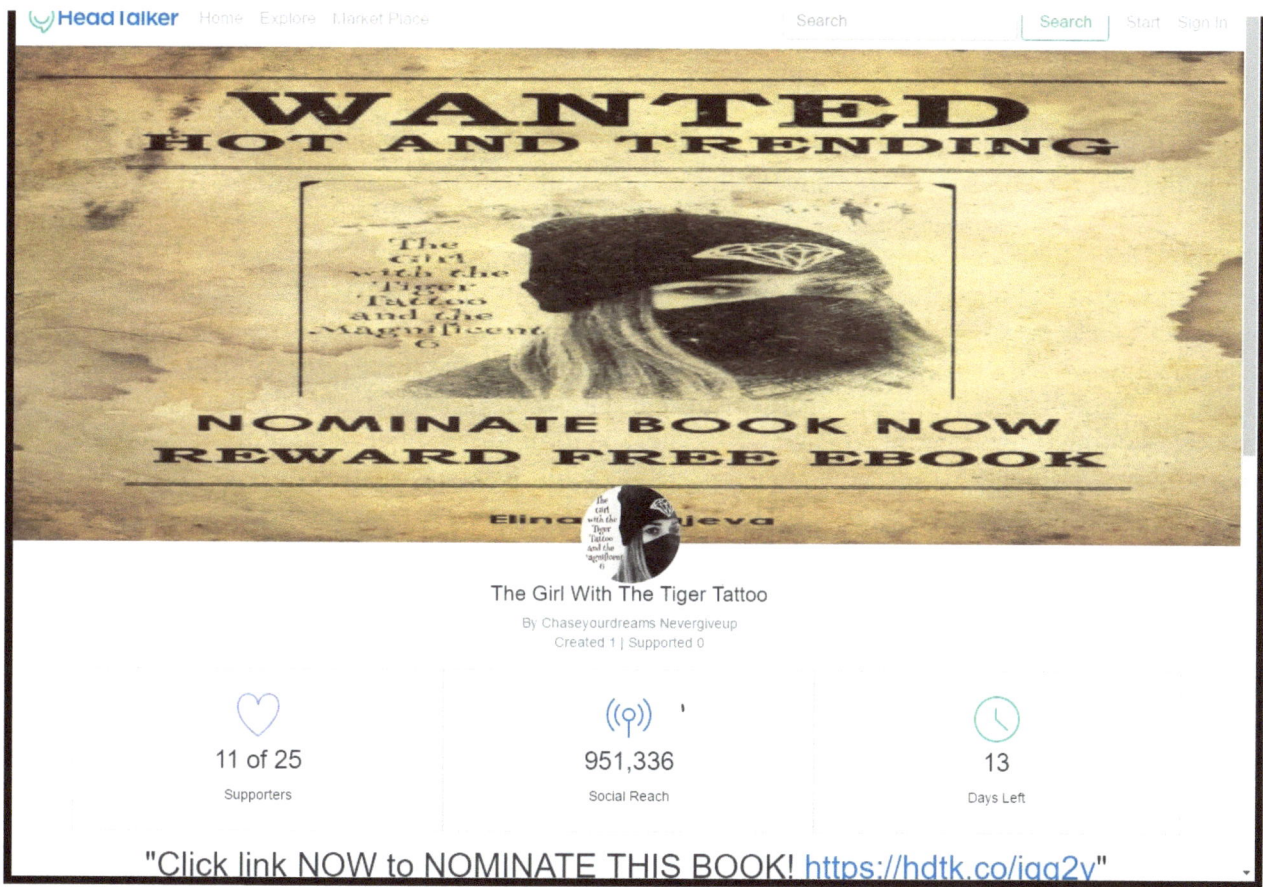

Go to Headtalker website and start a new campaign. Set the parameters accordingly, this is your initial wave and should run for only 5-7 days to give you enough to gather the minimum required number of supporters. The initial wave should be in the next 5 -7 days just after launch of the campaign. It can be shorter but ideally make it longer 7 days. This will also give your supporters time to relate to your book so that they will support you again when you launch the second and third Headtalker waves. Once you have started a Headtalker campaign you will automatically get some supporters. Wait for the next day. If you haven't reached 25 supporters, then its time you start asking for people's support. Go to Headtalker and check all; previous post and campaigns by authors. Look for the ones that had recently ended. Click on each member who has supported that campaign and get their information. Most people on Headtalker they have either a Facebook or twitter account. You can only register via a twitter account, a Tumblr account and a LinkedIn account. The most common are Facebook and twitter. After checking their information look up for them on either Facebook or twitter. Send them a message, inform them that you are running a Headtalker campaign and you are short of supporters. Explain that you are promoting your book in the hope that you will get a publishing contract after 30 days. You would appreciate it if they can support you. Be short and to the point. Calculate how many you need and send that figure plus 5 more in case some don't get your messages. When you have achieved the required number of supporters then forget about this wave. The date when the campaign ends depending on the number of supporter you got should be on the fifth day. That's when they release the messages to everyone in the account of the supporters. People all over the country or world will see and share your message. This will drive and divert enormous numbers of supporter and potential customers to your website. If they have an Amazon account, they will be able to nominate your book straight away. You will notice the impact after one or two days.

Open one Headtalker account with either Facebook or twitter and the second Elina's-Tsunami-Wave-Effect wave open using the other account. Same day open another Headtalker campaign using the other account you have haven't used for the initial Elina's-Tsunami-Wave-Effect wave.

Planning and launching Elina's-Tsunami-Wave-Effect wave two

This should be launched the same day as the Initial wave but us ea. different account name as well. Set this to be after two weeks. Increase the number of supporters to 50 or 100 but be realistic assess how many supporters you got the first time without soliciting for Initial Elina's-Tsunami-Wave-Effect wave one. Guess using that information how many supporters you are cable of getting. Please note that if you don't get the minimal number of supporters your promotional campaign won't be launched by Headtalker. So, be realistic unless if you know that you can get more supporters through soliciting.

Planning the Elina's-Tsunami-Wave-Effect wave three.

 This can be done at the same time just after starting wave one and two but you must use a different account either Tumblr or LinkedIn. Don't use the Facebook or twitter account. Each account for each campaign don't forget that. This should be bigger than the first and the second but again be realistic you don't want to end up failing to secure enough supporters that they will end up cancelling your campaign. The minimum number you put down will depend on your skills and other factors as well. If you can ask people to support you then do so.

Planning the Elina's-Tsunami-Wave-Effect wave four or final wave.

The for the fourth and final Wave the real big Elina's-Tsunami-Wave-Effect you must use Thunderclap. You will need 100 supporters and if you cannot meet the minimum number of supporters you will not be able to run the campaign. You must work hard trying to find supporters. Start the campaign application on day one. Go to Thunderclap and look for already completed campaigns and those about to end soon and contact as manly as you can during the first week. Explain your reasons why you need their help. Tell them something about your book give them the link and ask if they can help you give them time to decide and here chase after a day or two. It's not easy to have 100suporters. Go on face book they have a Thunderclap group post your book in there and ask for supporters. Give them the link to your Thunderclap campaign. Make sure you check the number of supporters you have by the end of the first week. Once you have reached the minimum number required then you can relax. You can use your four account to support your campaigns.

 Dos and Don'ts

Don't put the minimum number of supporters required very high because if you cannot get enough supporters your campaign won't be run.

Don't forget to check by end of the first week if you have gathered enough supporters for the big and final Elina's-Tsunami-Wave-Effect wave. Check also for the minimum number of supporters for all the other waves. Generate new short links to the link you will be emailed by Amazon. Use the different links for each Elina's-Tsunami-Wave-Effect phase. This is important.

The day your campaign will end is the day the Headtalker or the Thunderclap officials will send your message to thousands of people on Facebook, twitter, LinkedIn or Tumblr. So, on that day don't spend time on your account looking for supporters. It's ideally not to ask for support the day before and the next two days after your campaign ended. This is because the whole Facebook or twitter will be filled with your adverts. You don't want to overcrowd the internet and cause problems. On these two days, you relax and don't send any emails, SMS asking for nominations. Anyone who receives your promotional advert will automatically share these as well.

After securing the minimum number of supporters required then sit back and relax. Twit pieces of information from your book. Aim to build a strong base and retain audiences who will support you after the campaign has ended, don't get in the habit of rushing to ask for nominations. First day don't ask about nominations just introduce yourself. Let them know why you are running a camping and show that you want them to support you but you want them to make their own decision explain you will write again to find out what they think about your book. After a day or two them ask if you can rely on them for future support if they are there, write this down. You will need their votes in week 3 or 4. Ask them to share your posts with their friends and in groups they support.

I couldn't get enough support on Thunderclap so I relied on Headtalker for the final wave. I had put down a minimum number of supporters as 25 but surprisingly I ended up with 128 supporters with a social reach of over 1.3 million. This was my last and final Elina's-Tsunami-Wave-Effect wave to gather enough supporters and a solid fan base. This was exciting. 1.3million people all seeing my promotional campaign, I just thought yes this is exactly what I am looking for.

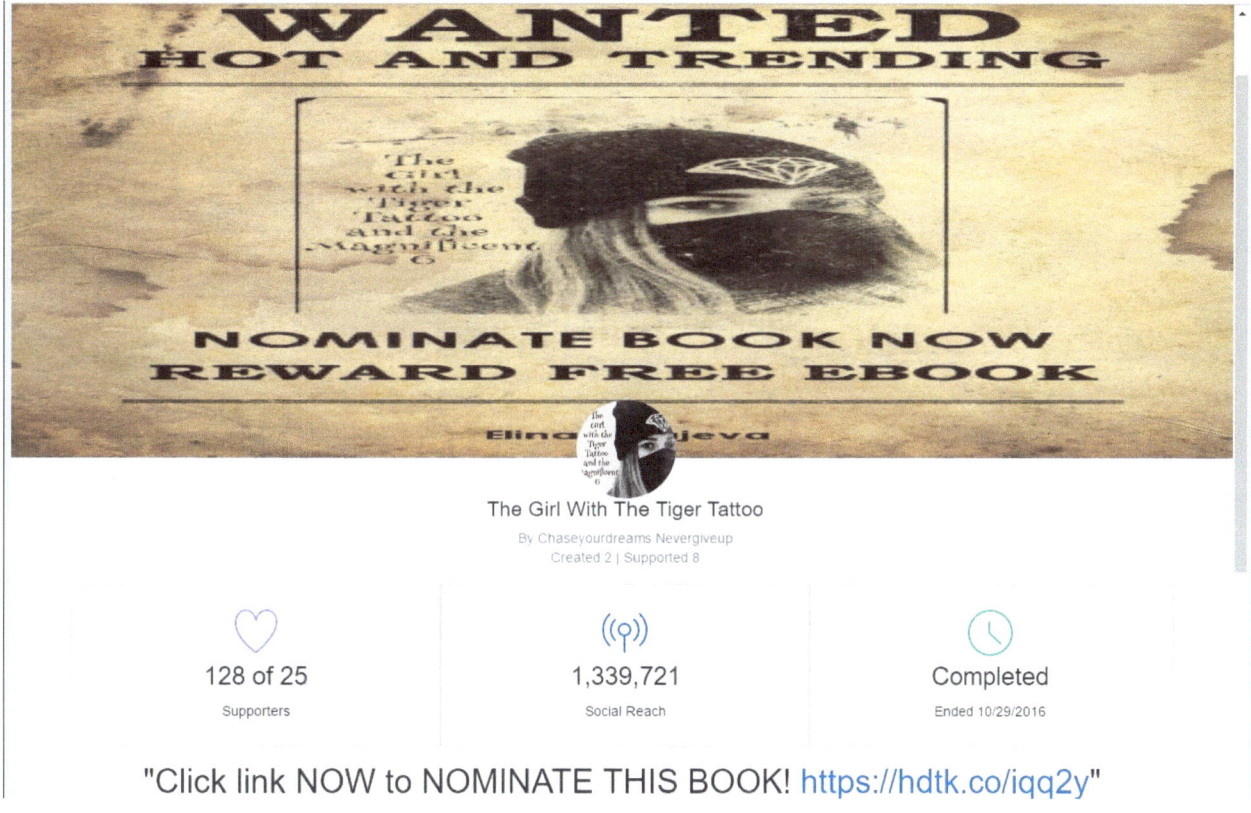

"Click link NOW to NOMINATE THIS BOOK! https://hdtk.co/iqq2y"

I had planned to use Thunderclap for the Final Elina's-Tsunami-Wave-Effect wave but I couldn't get enough supporters and I just didn't want to risk it. This is my final wave campaign on Thunderclap, see below image I had only 5 supporters out of 100. I just had no time to ask for supporters as I had other commitments. The potential social reach of this campaign was 61 887. This means that ideally this message could have been sent and seen and shared by all these people. Also, note that depending on how busy and crowded the platform is, sometime they send out your promotional message even if you haven't accumulated enough support for your campaign.

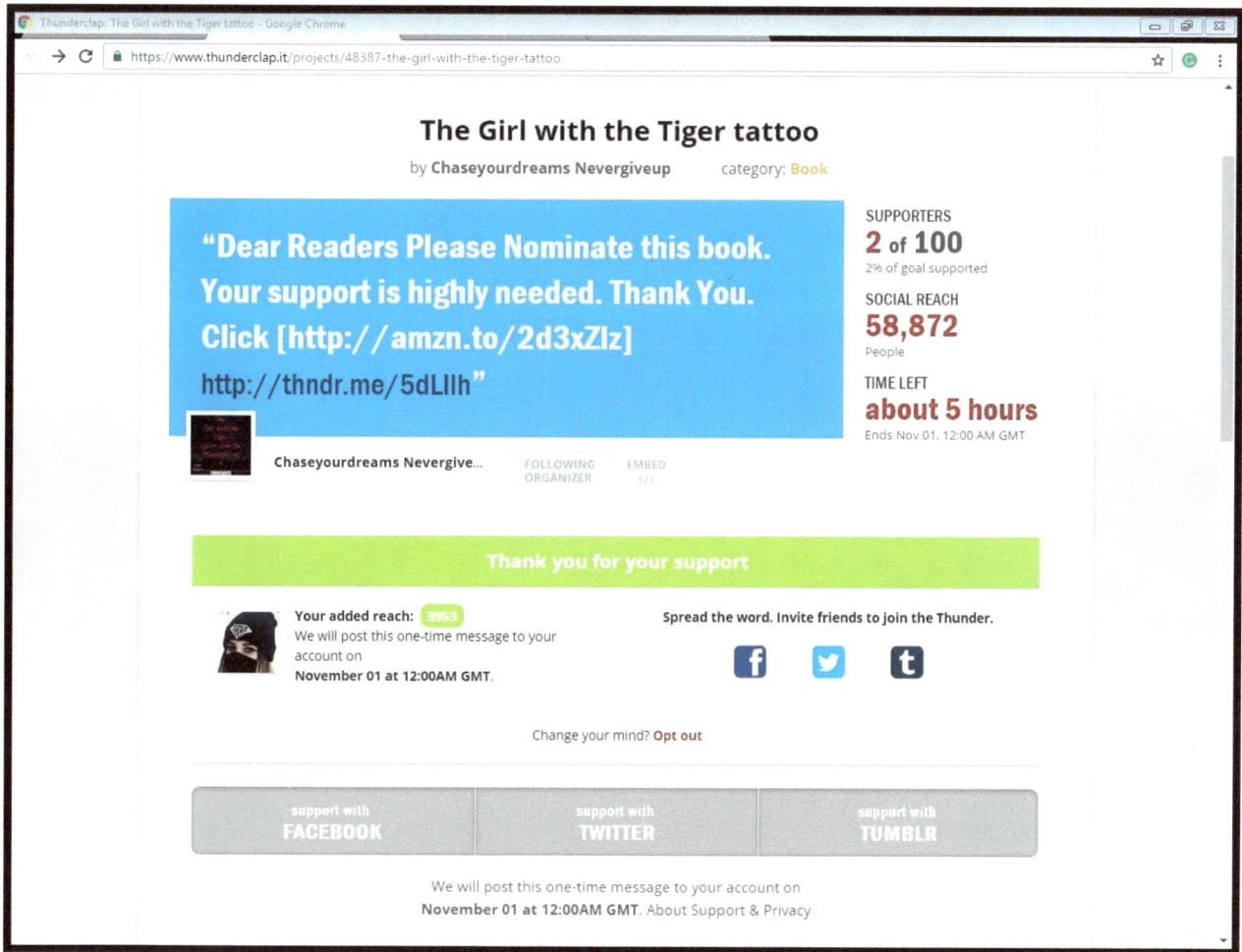

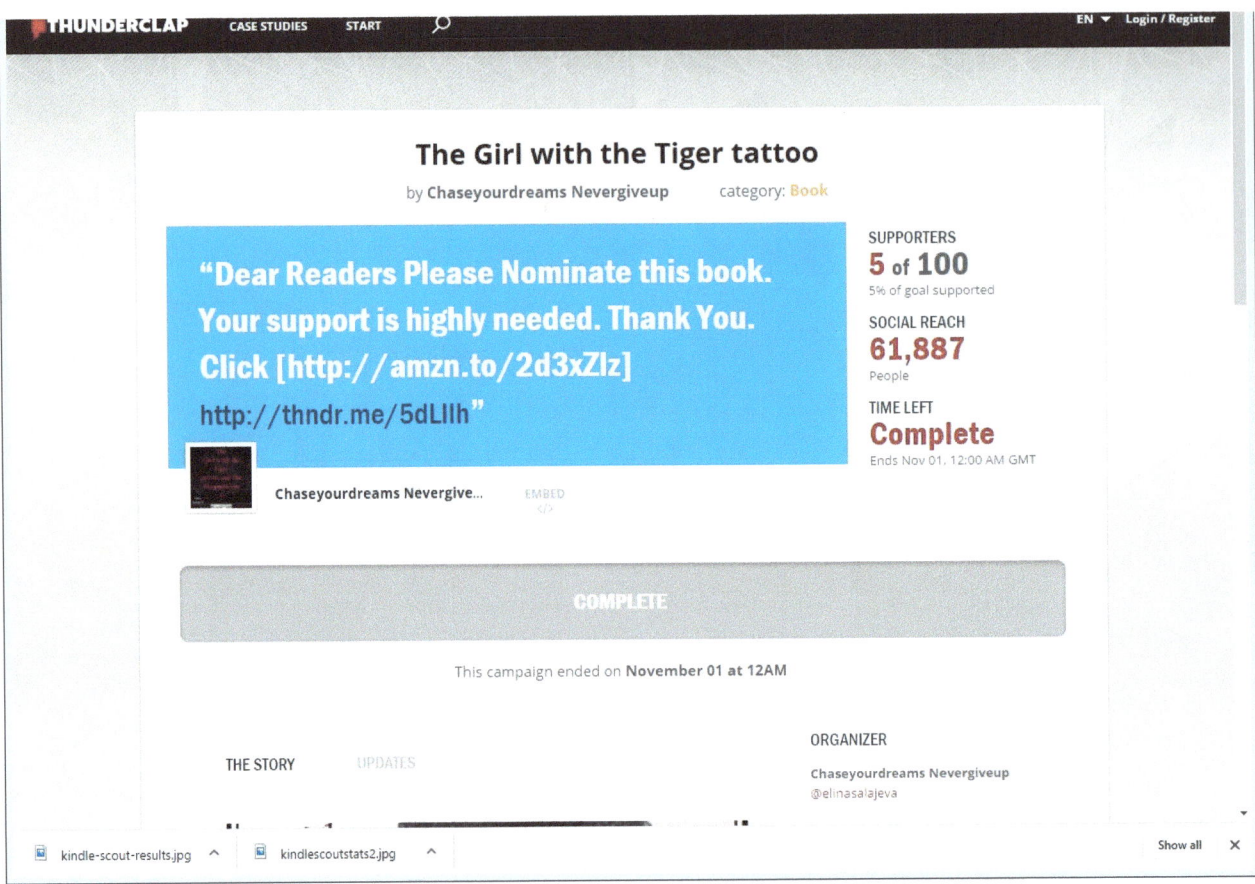

Hours in Hot and Trending per day: The Hot and Trending idea and its relevance or as an indicator of your performance.

Per Amazon Kindle Scout this indicator will give you a rough idea on the popularity of your book among the readers and how the book is doing. This is great way to measure your efforts as your campaign goes. There is no general guideline on how they measure this but I think it's worth it to look at this in some details. I think it's a good idea for your book to be in the hot and trending in the middle of your campaign. The reason being that if your book is hot in the week will it still be hot in the last week before your campaign ends. Can you generate a buzz that last that long. Or I should ask that is it a real buzz? This is the big question. "How far will the hotness and trending last? Is it for real? Or it's like a spirit drink that evaporates as soon as you open the bottle? Nothing wrong for your book to be hot and trending from the very first day but if you can control it I would prefer the book to be very hot from mid campaign or the third week enough to be strong and promising. Unless if you had already established loyal readers and followers of your work I think any quick buzz might not be real and therefore could be misleading. If your book is hot and trending alone without the necessary page view count, then it won't mean a lot. I have seen graphs where the book was hot and trending from the word go but because traffic to the Amazon website was minimum that person was not awarded a contract. The hot and trending figures should be supported by a strong page view count for one to be guaranteed a contract.

Look at an example below. There is no clear link between the number of campaign page views per day and the hours in hot and trending and the decision to offer you a contract. In the example below the person concerned was not awarded a contract despite the book being in Hot and trending for all the

Hours in Hot & Trending per day

The Hot & Trending list can give you a sense of your book's popularity with readers.

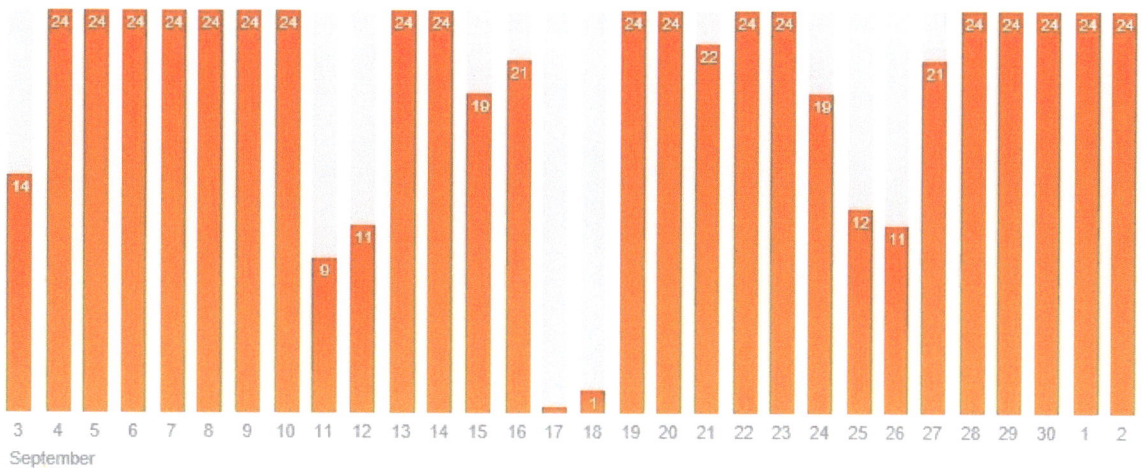

Campaign page views per day

Tracking daily campaign page views can help you monitor the effectiveness of your efforts.

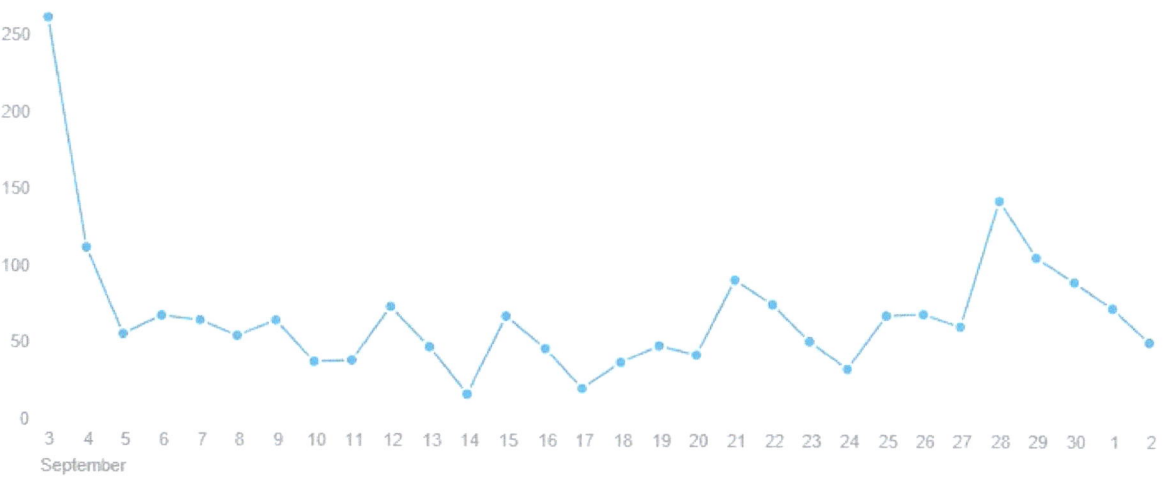

campaign. I think the hot and trending is just a guideline as to how you are performing and how popular your book is but what counts the most is the number of people you are ready to make that "ghost purchase". In mean people who click the link and visit your page. People can talk about your book but can are they prepared to make that purchase or it's just a buzz for the sake of a buzz.

They say put your money where your mouth is, I think that phrase is relevant here. You can trust someone who will say I follow you and buy your book than someone who will agree but never actual buy your book.

In some cases, there are good links between the hot and trending and the campaign page views per day. If you look at the graph below you will also see that there is only a relation between the hot and trending graph and the campaign page views per day in the first week in between despite an increase of page views mid- campaign the hot and trending remained low. The hours in hot and trending rose at the end of the campaign but the page views remained low at the end. The person concerned did not get the contract. So, it seems the hot and trending hours has little or no effect on its own on whether one gets a contract or not.

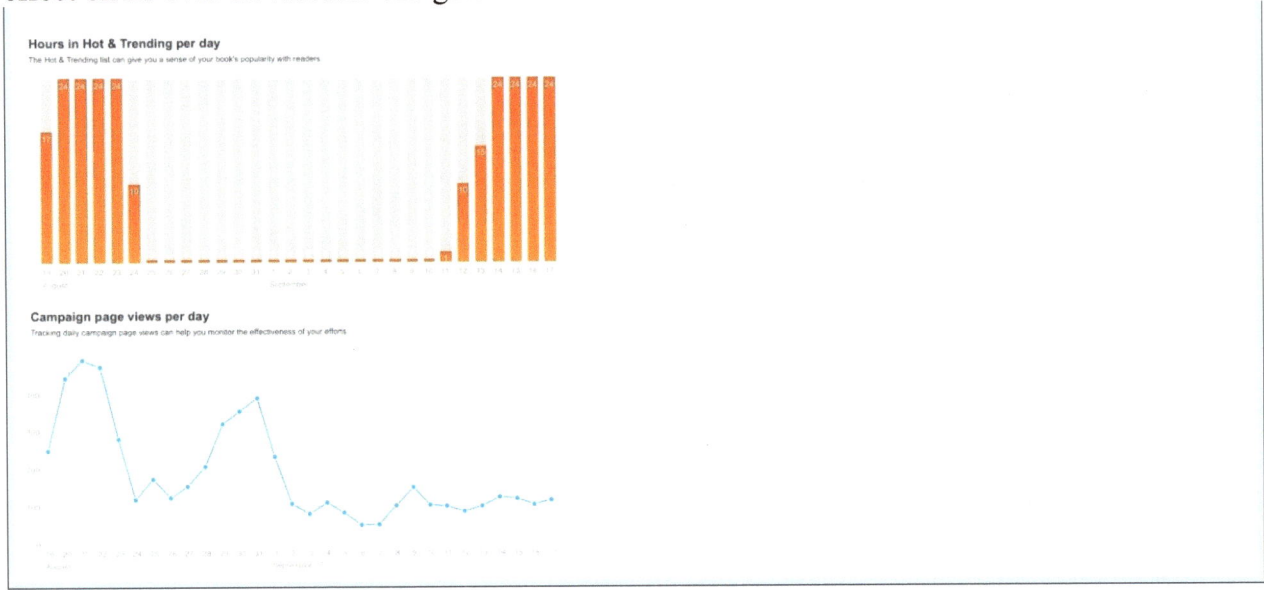

The person below did not get a contract despite the book being in hot and trending for most of the time especially at the end of the campaign. The reason being that he or she had very few page visits at the end of the campaign.

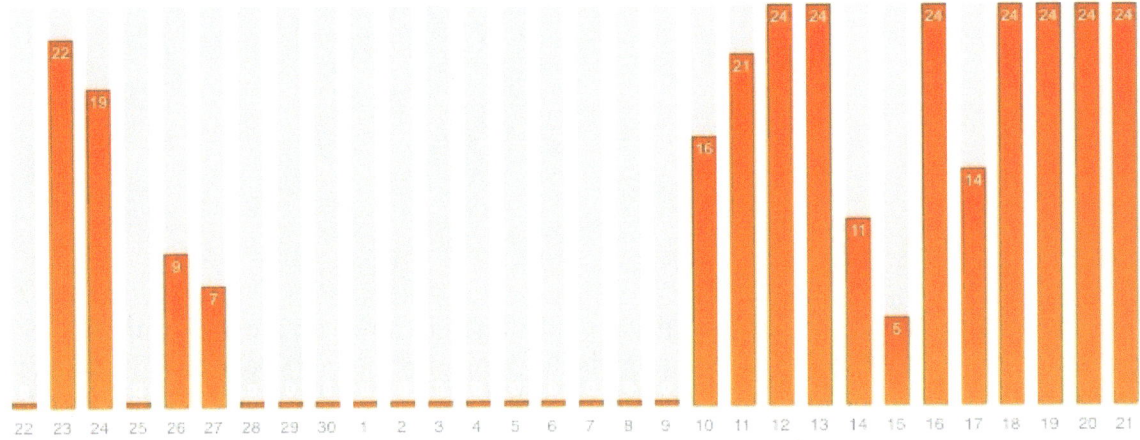

Now let's look at a case where the hot and trending hours are linked to the number of page views. In this case the author had a healthy campaign with peaks throughout until the end of the campaign as well. Check the graph below. The last day of the campaign the page views rose which is a good sign and I think this was a strong reason to award the person a contract. The book was hot throughout and the peaks in between made the case for a contract more favourable.

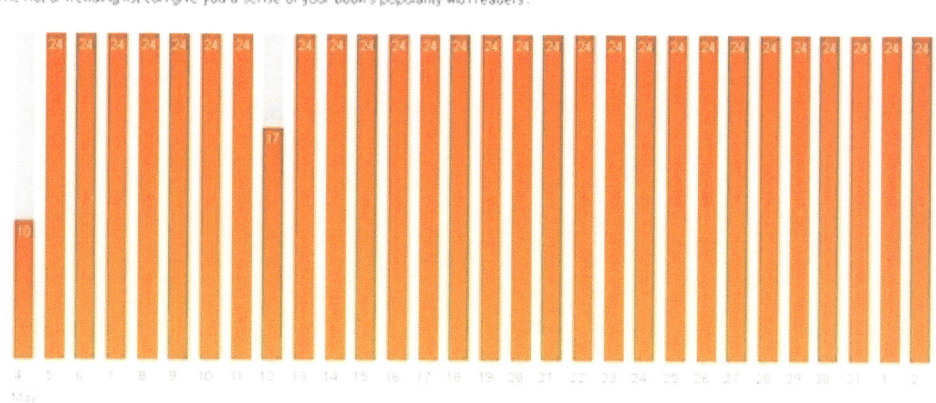

The Hot & Trending list can give you a sense of your book's popularity with readers.

To conclude on this topic, I would say that you need to have a sound page views count throughout the campaign and it would be ideal to have peaks at the end of the campaign rather than at the beginning. There is no clear relationship between the hours in hot and trending and the page count and the awarding of the contract. I have dwelt much on the Elina's-Tsunami-Wave-Effect wave method as a way of boosting page views at the end of the campaign where it counts. The hot and trending is something you cannot control so I wouldn't worry much about that. You can control or influence the number of people who will visit your website and click the link and nominate you through your efforts and I personally think that what matters the most.

Aim to increase the page views as these are the ones that will turn into sales. When your book is due for publishing at the end of the campaign and you have a lot of page views at the end of the campaign I think these will reflect the sales you will make. You will have an already waiting strong fan base. You have built the foundation for the past week and now it's time to reap the benefits.

Now let's look at the campaign trail.

There are so many ways you can advertise and promote your book. There are hundreds of websites out there where you can place your post for free. If your budget is tight you can use all your social networks Facebook, twitter, Myspace, Tumblr, Okru, Weibo, youtube, LinkedIn, WordPress etc. The idea is to plan. Choose where and when your post should appear at what websites. Don't overflood the internet or your social network with the same post every day. You will lose your image. Instead plan everything. Get a calendar and mark which date your posts will appear say on Facebook. The idea is to have two or three different set of posts or adverts. Have your book cover for the Facebook account from say Monday to Wednesday and another related picture from Thursday to Sunday. If you put one advert say of your book cover on Monday on Facebook, then on twitter on Monday put a different cover or post and the rotate. What was on twitter on Monday will be on Facebook from Thursday to Sunday. I will show you below what I mean. This is one of the promotional advert I used as an alternate to the book cover. This is part of the book cover. Like I was saying in the above chapters try to be very creative go out of your comfort zone. The readers are humans as well they get bored, they get fade up with repetitions, they want something new, something eye catching, something different. You don't want to be a Sustainer or a Dreamer nor a Planner, do you? You want to be the head the leader one day the rich person, right? This is how you do it. Strive to attract new followers and for those you have already aim to retain them. Be spontaneous.

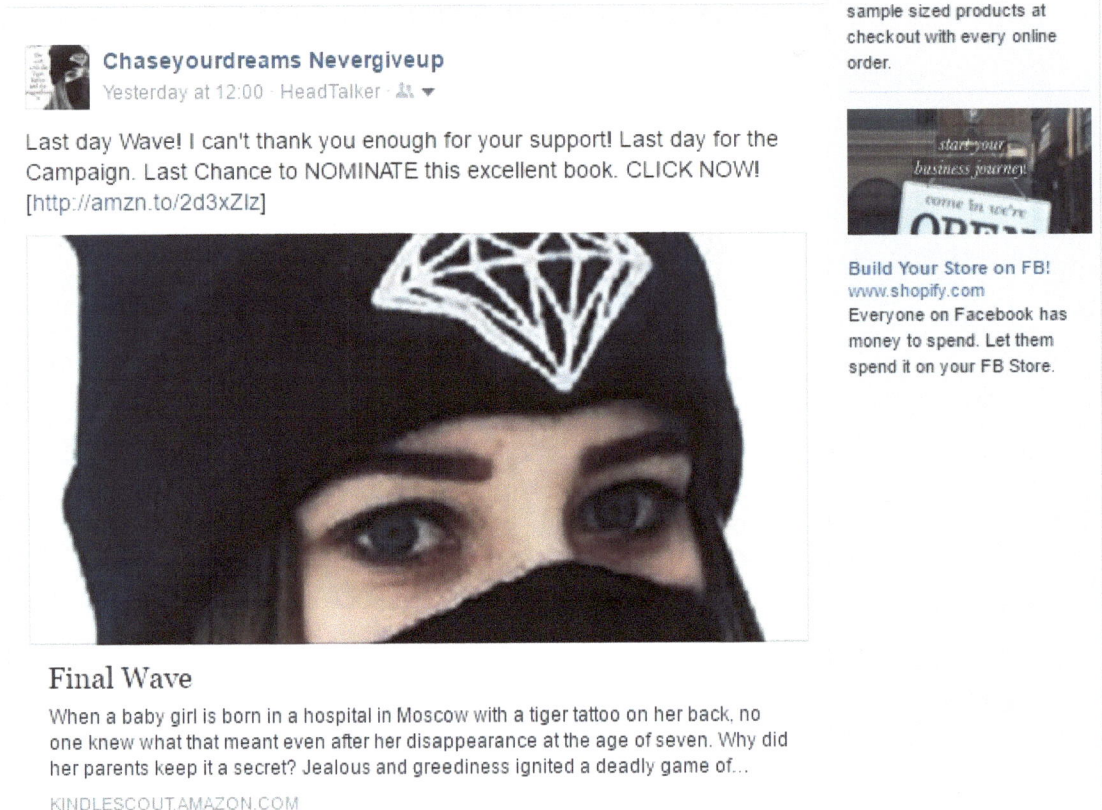

The other thing you should be aware of when promoting your book on Facebook is to be careful and clearly ask the potential supporters to visit the amazon kindle scout page by clicking the links rather than liking the Facebook page. The first time I launched my campaign on face book I had nearly 250 visit to the web page on my Facebook and people 222 like the Facebook page and never bothered clicking the link to my Kindle Scout page. Only a handful around 30 people were that curious. I woke the next day thinking I have smashed the Kindle Scout daily page views only to find out that only 33 where actually directed from Facebook. I had a 9,200% increase in traffic to my site after I launched my book. Try to avoid ambiguity especially if you are going to rely on Facebook for supporters.

In response, I tried to control how things goes, I didn't want to leave anything to chance. The idea is to try and control or influence the whole process, in other words make it predictable.

Chaseyourdreams Nevergiveup
28 October at 20:22 · 🌐 ▼

PLEASE Don't just like the page NOMINATE my book CLICK THE LINK!
Great Thank You!
3days to go. Make history nominate this book. Click link now
https://kindlescout.amazon.com/p/1N5BYLN9OGELY

The Girl With The Tiger Tattoo -
HeadTalker

Click link NOW to NOMINATE THIS BOOK!

HEADTALKER.COM

👍 Like   💬 Comment   ➤ Share

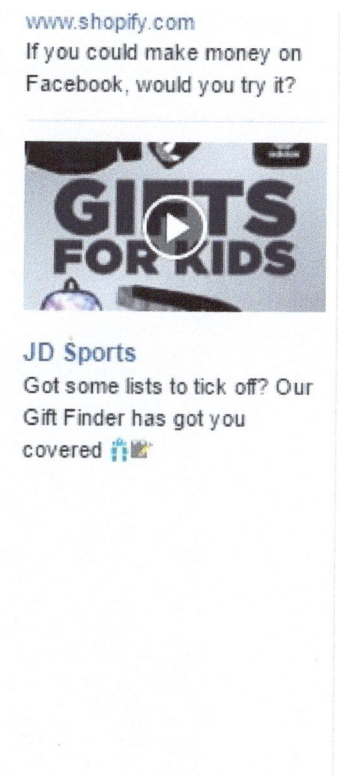
I ended up with three images or posts I can use for my campaign. The main cover had too much text so using this for adverts was a problem. I had to quickly design another one. I ended up with the one below which was superb as it was highly welcomed than I thought.

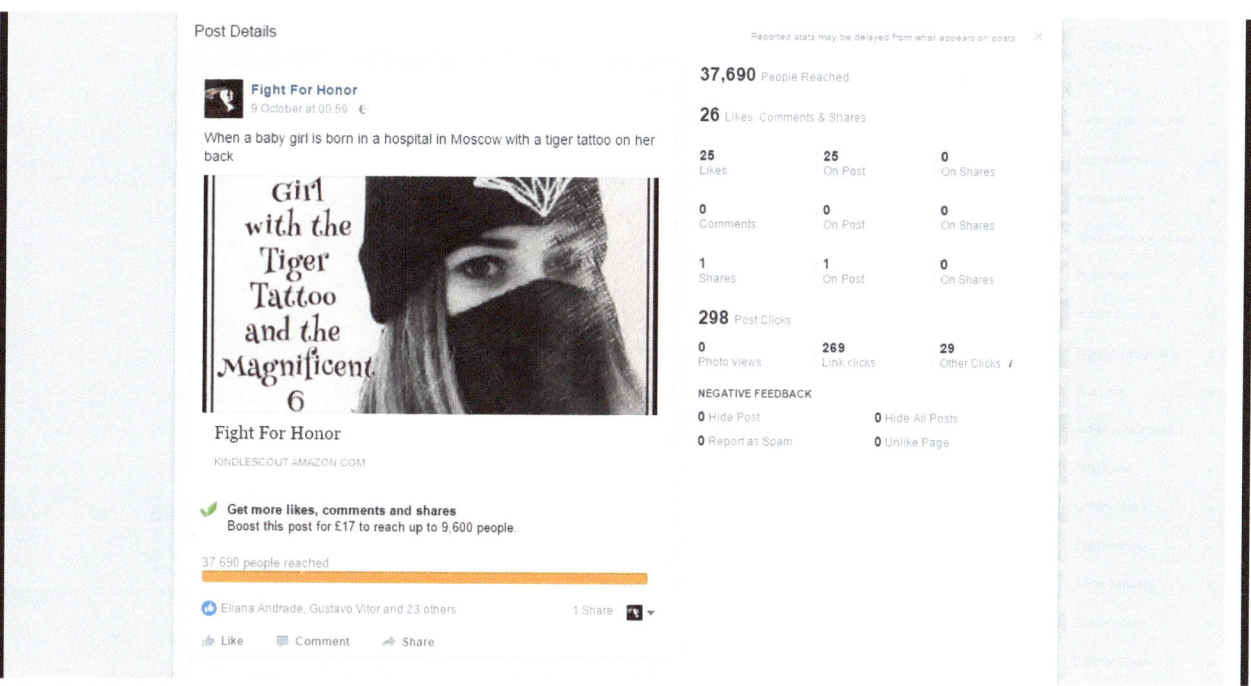

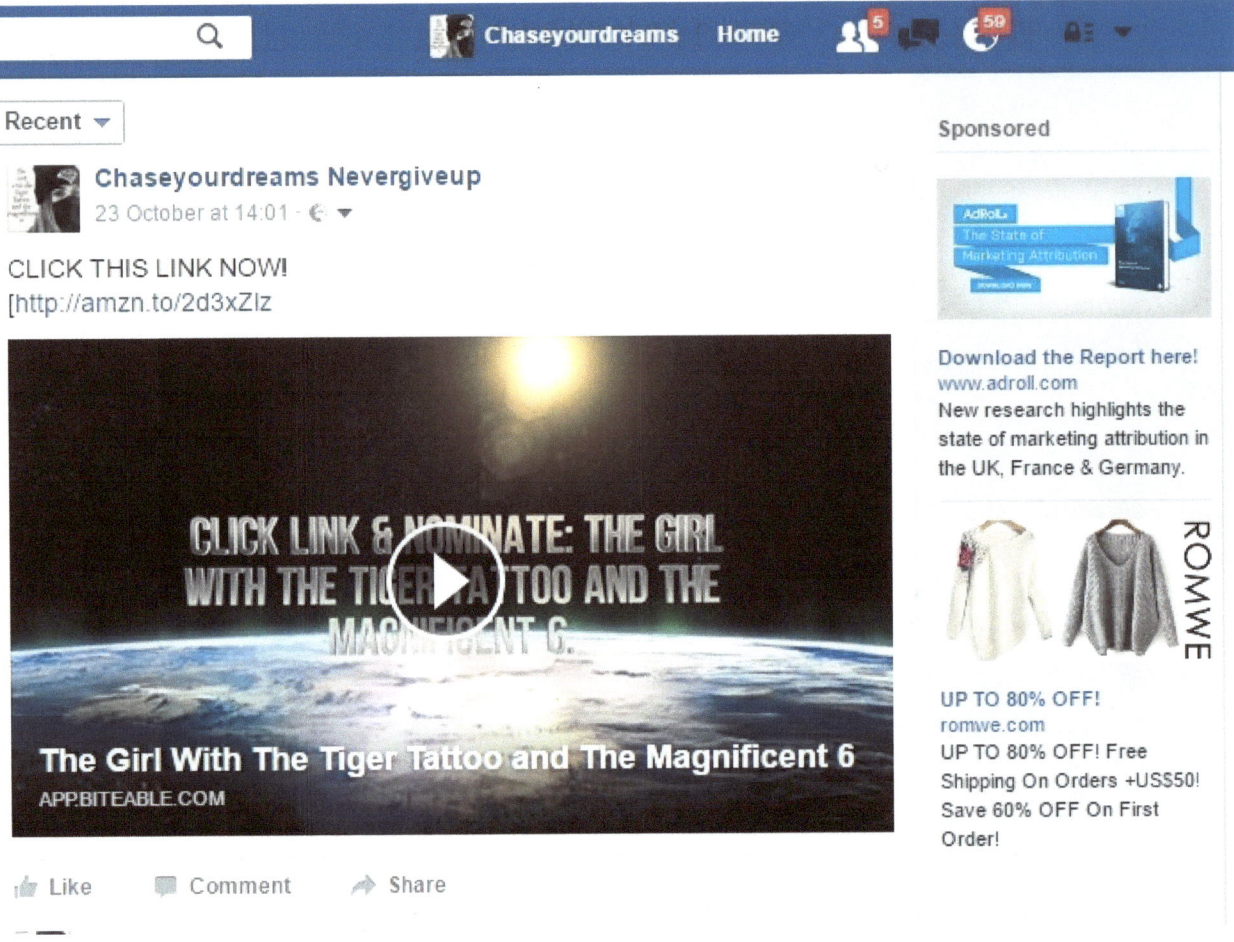

After the first two weeks, I started going out of my way being creative as I can be. This was fun, I had notifications on Facebook minute after minute that several people were liking my posts. I just though hey what's the hack I might as well show off. I research on how I can make a quite video that sends my message loud and clear. I found this site www.biteable.com. I opted for the intro short videos to create the video to my campaign. This was clear I think. The video was 30 seconds long. Short, cute and to the point. Click link and nominate my book. This helped bring in more supporters and week three just saw an increase in number of visitors to my Facebook and clicks to the links increased as well.

Another eye-catching advert that brought in supporters was the post below. I adopted this from the cowboy world where a wanted poster was used to find and identify the wanted man. This was funny and all these where used in the third week and for sure the support just kept growing with every day. People were making repeat visits and clicking likes to most of my post. I knew this was it. In week three I must start building that Tsunami ball that will explode in the last days see the graph.

Like I was saying at the beginning you are what you make yourself. Some of these things they want understanding and preparing for them. Never leave things to chance. You chase after the chance. Don't wait for the chance to come to you, what if doesn't, instead Chase Your Dreams Never Give Up.

[https://read.amazon.co.uk/kp/embed?asin=B01GOTXJE4&preview=newtab&linkCode=kpe&ref_=cm_sw_r_kb_dp_OpmgybEVDWYKM]

Be as creative as you can to attract more supporters and potential future customers stand out let everything about your profiles show that you mean business in the end you will be award that lucrative contract. $25000 in five years, $1500 cash advancement doing something you love honestly nothing can go wrong.

It's all up to you. If you want to be a Sustainer, a Dreamer, a Planner, a Modifier, a Practicalizer, an Innovator or a Challenger or even better a leader or the head. It's all up to you but it never hurts to be creative and to take a little bit of risks here and there.

What now?

I have worked hard to build a robust fan base nearly 23k strong (Facebook 3k, twitter 20k) and I think the future so far is brighter. I ended my campaign with a HUGE VERY JUICY 800 (807 to be precise) page views per day I think that's a record. I tried to find out if any one had ever had such high page views per day. The highest I have found so far had 600 page views per day but that person had to pay money to a certain website who did that for her or for him. If you want to enjoy the fun and don't have money to blow then follow my methods. These are tried and trusted methods guaranteeing you to win that lucrative contract, keep this book this is your holy grail of Amazon Kindle Scout.

I hope you enjoyed reading my book there are a lot of topics to cover but here I have illustrated the major issues. This will turn out to be your best purchase so far.

Bless!

Buy my book also @AMAZON it's a great read; *The Girl with the Tiger Tattoo and the Magnificent 6.*

In the future, I am planning to turn this book into a movie, they say the sky is the limit there are endless opportunities.

The End!